THE UNDERGROUND
RAILROAD
in
DELAWARE

THE UNDERGROUND
RAILROAD
— *in* —
DELAWARE

Michael Morgan

THE
History
PRESS

Published by The History Press
Charleston, SC
www.historypress.com

First published 2023

Manufactured in the United States

ISBN 9781467152419

Library of Congress Control Number: 2022950084

CONTENTS

PREFACE

In the years before the Civil War, freedom seekers used the Underground Railroad, a loose network of dark trails and safe houses, to escape the bonds of slavery. In many areas, these routes have been documented, but in Delaware, they have mostly been ignored. *The Underground Railroad in Delaware* is an attempt to correct this oversight and to recognize the vital role the First State played in assisting fugitives to reach freedom. This book is drawn mostly from works published in the nineteenth century, such as the autobiography of Frederick Douglass, which he revised twice; Sarah Bradford's two works on Harriet Tubman; William Still's *Underground Rail Road Records*; and newspapers from that period. *The Underground Railroad in Delaware* constructs a framework that may serve as a guide to further research drawn from family traditions and keepsake documents.

It has been just over a century and a half since slavey was abolished in the United States, and during those years, some conventions of spelling and grammar have changed. In direct quotations, punctuation that does affect the meaning has been modernized. In the nineteenth century, many works that quoted Black Americans recorded these words in a heavy dialect, using "dem" for "them," "ob" for "of" and so forth. The words of white speakers were recorded accent free, even though many of them spoke with thick southern, Irish, New England and other accents. This practice was discriminatory at best and racist at worst, and it amounted to verbal blackface. Therefore, all such accounts in this book are recorded accent free. Likewise, the n-word was freely used in the nineteenth century, and to reproduce it would grant legitimacy to its use. The word is too odious to be used in this book, and it has been replaced by n—r to remain true to the nineteenth-century sources and to indicate the word should not be repeated.

I would like to thank my son Tom and his wife, Karla, for their support and technical assistance. Finally, I would like to thank my wife, Madelyn, for her constant editorial advice and support. She read every word in this book numerous times and spent countless hours correcting my spelling, punctuation and grammar. Without her help, encouragement and suggestions, this book would not have been possible.

PROLOGUE

Let him be a fugitive in a strange land—a land given up to be the hunting ground for slaveholders—whose inhabitants are legalized kidnappers—where he is every moment subject to the terrible liability of being seized upon by his fellowmen, as the hideous crocodile seize upon his prey!
—Frederick Douglass[1]

THE STEEL FAMILY: 1805

The Delmarva Peninsula, bounded by the Chesapeake Bay to the west and the Delaware Bay and the Atlantic Ocean to the east, is a low, broad peninsula that contains parts of Maryland, Virginia and the entire of the state of Delaware. Caroline County is the only county on Maryland's Eastern Shore that is landlocked (it does not have a waterfront on the Chesapeake Bay), and it lacks the extensive marshy grasslands of the bayfront counties. Instead, Caroline County shares a long and straight border with Delaware, and on the ground, it was sometimes difficult to determine where Maryland ended and Delaware began—a question of dispute since the colonies were founded. In 1763, Charles Mason and Jeremiah Dixon were hired by the colonial leaders to survey the border, and they placed stone markers every mile to indicate the boundary line. But in the unsettled areas of the central Delmarva Peninsula, the markers were lost in the wilderness.

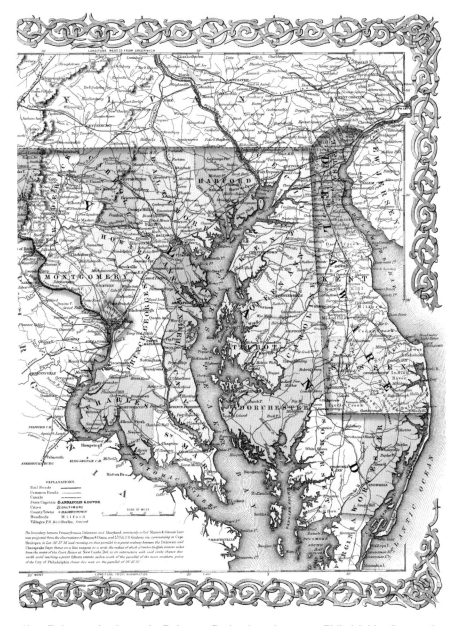

Above: Delaware dominates the Delmarva Peninsula and routes to Philadelphia. *Courtesy of the Delaware Public Archives.*

Opposite: Sidney Steel was an early passenger on the Delaware Underground Railroad. *From Still*, Underground Rail Road.

Delaware's border with Maryland did not matter much to Sidney as she pondered her family's escape. Sidney and her husband, Levin, were enslaved on a Caroline County farm, and as a young man, Levin had been beaten by an overseer using a maul that nearly broke his back and left him maimed for life. When Levin's master died, the plantation's enslaved people were inherited by his son. Fortunately, Levin was able to bargain with his new master. Levin swore, "I sooner die than stay a slave." Considering Levin's disability and determination, his new master set a reasonable price for his freedom, and he was allowed to work on outside jobs to accumulate the needed money. After several years of hard work, Levin had enough to purchase his freedom.

Once liberated, Levin moved to Greenwich, New Jersey, a township on the Delaware River where the river widens into the Delaware Bay. Although Levin left his family behind, he did not desert them. In New Jersey, Levin planned to free Sidney and the children. Levin's route from Caroline County to Greenwich, New Jersey, is not known, but the most direct path was overland through Delaware to Pearson's Cove (now Woodland Beach) on the Delaware River, which would have taken Levin about a day and a half if he were on foot. If he had a horse, he could have covered the thirty-five miles in a day. Levin was a free man with manumission papers, and he did not need to travel at night; this also would have quickened his travel. Once he reached Pearson's Cove, he would have needed a boat to cross the Delaware River, and at the time, oyster boats, fishing vessels and large sailing ships were common on the river. It is possible that Levin may have befriended a crewman aboard one of the smaller sailing vessels, or he may have paid someone to take him across the river to New Jersey.

It appears that Levin communicated with Sidney, but how much guidance he gave her is not known. He quite possibly laid out the route that she would take across Delaware to New Jersey. The details are unclear, but in 1805, Sidney gathered up their four children and set out for New Jersey and freedom.

When Sidney's owner learned that the Steel family had fled, he was furious, and he hired a slave catcher to find them. A Black woman traveling with four young children would have been noticed, particularly if they had taken a boat across the Delaware River to Greenwich. The slave catchers located Sidney and her four children in New Jersey and dragged them back to their owner's farm in Caroline County; there, Sidney was locked in a garret every night to keep her from running away again.[2]

Fred Bailey: Circa 1825

Fred Bailey was born around 1818 in Tuckahoe, Talbot County, Maryland, less than a dozen miles from the Steel cabin. The exact day and year of Bailey's birth are unknown. Bailey recalled, "By far, the larger part of the slaves know as little of their ages as horses know of theirs, and it is the wish of most masters within my knowledge to keep their slaves ignorant."[3] His mother was Harriet Bailey, and his father was a white man, perhaps his owner. As was common, Fred was separated from his mother when he was an infant. Frequently in that part of Maryland, enslaved mothers were hired out to other plantations, and their children were placed in the care of older women who were too old for field labor. In this way, slave owners sought to destroy all family ties of those they held in bondage.

Fred could remember seeing his mother only four or five times. She came to visit him only at night. She left before morning, and Fred never saw her by the light of day. Harriet died when Bailey was about seven years old. She was gone before he knew anything about her illness, death or burial.[4]

Bailey's master was a man named Anthony, who was generally called "Captain" Anthony, presumably a title he acquired by sailing on the Chesapeake Bay. Unlike Caroline County, Talbot County had many coves and inlets on the Chesapeake, and many of its people, white and Black, were tied to the water.

As a young child, Fred slept on the dirt floor of a little rough closet that was separated from the kitchen by a crudely made door of loose-fitting slats. Early one morning, Fred was awakened by a commotion in the kitchen. Peeking through the gaps in the unplaned door slats, Fred could see Captain Anthony dragging Fred's aunt Hester into the kitchen.[5] Hester was a beautiful young woman who had a boyfriend on a nearby farm, and she had slipped out late one night without her master's permission. When Captain Anthony discovered this, he was enraged, and he meant to teach her a lesson. While Fred watched from his cubbyhole, Captain Anthony stripped Hester's clothes off from her neck to her waist and tied her hands with a strong rope. Anthony ordered her to stand on a bench that was beneath a large hook driven into a rafter above her. When he tied

Enslaved people were hung from the rafters to facilitate flogging. *From Still*, Underground Rail Road.

her hands to the hook, Hester stood, helpless, extending her arms over her head and standing on the ends of her toes. Anthony announced, "Now, you damned bitch, I'll learn you how to disobey my orders."[6] Rolling up his sleeves, Anthony picked up a heavy cowskin, a whip common in the slaveholding states. Made of untanned, dried ox hide, the inch-thick handle of the cowskin was as hard as a piece of oak, but as the whip tapered toward the end of its three- or four-foot length, it was flexible. Painted red, blue or green, the cowskin, when swung by an experienced hand, made a whistling sound, and a single blow could gash the flesh and make blood flow. Considered worse than the cat-o-nine tails because the force of its blow was concentrated in single area, the cowskin was the weapon of choice for slave-driving overseers.[7] Fred, trembling in his cabinet hiding place, watched as Anthony completed the preparations for the scourging. Then the cowhide began to whistle, Hester shrieked, Anthony cursed and the warm red blood dripped to the floor.

The memory of that day was seared into Fred's memory. "I was quite a child, but I well remember it. I never shall forget whilst I remember anything. It was the first of a long series of such outrages, of which I was doomed to be a witness and a participant. It struck me with awful force. It was the blood-stained gate, the entrance to the hell of slavery through which I was about to pass. It was the most terrible spectacle."[8]

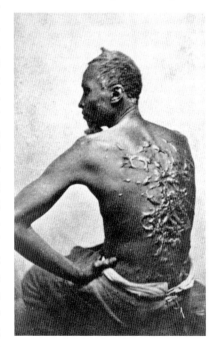

This was not the last time Anthony flogged Hester. Many years later, Fred recalled, "I have often been awakened at the dawn of day by the most heart-rending shrieks of an own aunt of mine, whom he used to tie up to a joist and whip upon her naked back till she was literally covered with blood. No words, no tears, no prays from his gory victim seemed to move his iron heart for its bloody purpose. The louder she screamed, the harder he whipped, and where the blood ran fastest, there he whipped the longest."[9]

Many freedom seekers bore the scars of the cowhide whipping. *Courtesy of the Library of Congress.*

Common mode of whipping with the paddle.

Slave owners sometimes used a wooden paddle to beat their enslaved people. *Courtesy of the Library of Congress.*

ARAMINTA "MINTY" ROSS: 1844

One of the enslaved people who was confused about her date of birth was Araminta Ross. Called "Minty," she was born around 1822 to enslaved parents, Harriet "Rit" and Benjamin Ross, on the Dorchester County plantation of Anthony Thompson. South of Talbot and Caroline Counties, Dorchester's southern border was formed by the Nanticoke River that ran deep into Delaware.

Once, when serving as a house servant, Minty stole a lump of sugar, and her master became so enraged that Minty ran away and hid in a pigsty for several days, fighting the hogs for scraps of food. Finally, she returned home to face the beating that awaited her. The whipping was so bad that she suffered broken ribs and lifelong scars.[10] At the time, Minty was six or seven years old.

When Minty was around thirteen years old, she was hired out as a field hand. One night, Minty accompanied the farm's cook to a small general store, where she was inadvertently caught in the middle of an altercation between an enslaved man and his overseer. The enslaved man went to the store without permission, and the overseer followed him. When the overseer arrived, he swore that he would whip the enslaved man and called on the others in the store to help tie the enslaved man up. Minty refused, but when the enslaved man began to run, she stood by the doorway, and the overseer picked up a two-pound weight from a measuring scale and threw it at the enslaved man. The weight missed the enslaved man and hit Minty in the head.[11] The weight drove part of Minty's shawl into her head and probably fractured her skull.[12] They carried Minty, bleeding and going in and out of consciousness, home to the slave quarters and laid her on the seat next to a loom. She remained there until the next day with no further medical attention. She was then ordered back to the fields, where she worked with sweat and blood rolling down her face so thick that she could not see.

The injury left a scar on her head and caused permanent damage to her brain. She would sometimes fall asleep in the middle of a conversation, and she told others that when she slipped into unconsciousness, they should not be alarmed, as she would soon revive after three or four minutes and continue the conversation where she left off. Deeply religious, Minty would also experience vivid dreams and voices that she interpreted as prophetic visions that she was compelled to follow.[13]

For the next several years, Minty matured into a young woman, and despite her head injury, she earned a reputation as a hard worker. She made an arrangement with her master for a set yearly fee to be hired out to others who needed labor. Minty was allowed to keep the excess of the yearly payment made to her master. With some of that money, she was able to buy a team of oxen, which enabled her to do more work and earn additional money. She hauled lumber, plowed fields, set traps for muskrats and did all the work expected of a field hand.[14]

At that time, the Black population in that part of the Eastern Shore was mixed between enslaved and free. By the time Minty was around twenty-two years old, she had met John Tubman. They fell in love and were married in 1844. When she took John's last name, she also changed her first name, perhaps in honor of her mother, and Minty Ross became Harriet Tubman.[15]

SURVEYING THE ROUTE

Run away from the subscriber, a Negro man, named Liverpool; he is a tall slim fellow, has a very small head and face, long small legs....I am apprehensive he is gone to the northward.
—Maryland Gazette, *April 15, 1746*[16]

1619: Two Beginnings

The Underground Railroad in Delaware had its roots in Jamestown, Virginia, the earliest permanent English settlement in what eventually became the United States. The year after the English settlers established Jamestown in 1607, Captain John Smith (with his trademark full red beard) and fourteen other colonists took a small boat and sailed across the Chesapeake Bay to begin the first European exploration of the Delmarva Peninsula. After reaching the Eastern Shore, Smith doggedly made his way northward until he entered a river the Natives called Kuskarawaok, now known as the Nanticoke. Smith's small boat navigated the twists and turns of the Nanticoke River until he reached what is now Sussex County, Delaware, where he had several encounters—some peaceful, some not—with Natives. After exploring the river and some of the surrounding territory, Smith and his party headed down the Nanticoke River out of Delaware and into the Chesapeake Bay, where he continued to explore the rivers and creeks flowing out of the Delmarva Peninsula. Several years later, Smith published an account of his adventures in the New World, and the Europeans, with their enslaved Africans and free Black settlers, followed in Smith's wake to colonize southwest Delaware.[17]

John Smith had returned to England to write his memoirs by 1619, when the House of Burgesses met for the first time. This began the tradition that each English colony—and eventually, the United States—should have an assembly of representatives of the people as an integral part of its government. It was not a full-blown twenty-first-century democracy. Not everyone could vote, and individual rights were yet to be established, but it was a start, and representative government continues to evolve in the twenty-first century.

Also in 1619, the year before the *Mayflower* arrived at Plymouth Rock, the privateer *White Lyon*, with a number of Africans aboard, docked at Point Comfort, several miles from Jamestown, near the entrance to the Chesapeake Bay. Unlike the Pilgrims, who willingly braved the hazards of crossing the Atlantic to start a new life in America, the Black men and women on the *White Lyon* had been captured during a war in Africa, thrust into chains and, along with over three hundred other captives, carried aboard a Portuguese ship bound for Mexico. When the ship reached the Bay of Campeche, it was attacked by the *White Lyon*, and a number of these Africans were taken aboard. And in August 1619, the *White Lyon* sailed into the Chesapeake Bay and docked at Point Comfort. The Virginia colonists bought twenty or so of the captured human cargo, and in the same year that democracy was begun in America, the first enslaved people arrived in the Jamestown colony.[18] Although they were involuntarily bound to their masters, it appears that their service was to be for a set period of time, as specified in a contract or "indenture" that required them to work to cover the cost of their purchase, plus their food and boarding. Sometimes, people became indentured servants willingly, but the Africans aboard the *White Lyon* were kidnapped into their positions against their will, and they should be considered "term slaves." Like democracy, slavery was an evolving institution, so by the time the Underground Railroad became active in Delaware, to be enslaved generally meant three things. First, unlike indentured servitude, apprenticeship and conviction, slavery was a lifelong condition from which there was little chance of lawful escape. Second, the enslaved were their master's chattel and could be bought and sold at will—this differed from serfs who were tied to the land. Usually thought of as a medieval institution, serfdom lasted in some European countries, such as Russia, well into the nineteenth century. Finally, slavery was a matriarchal institution. The status of an infant was determined by the status of their mother.

The Netherlands shared with England a vigorous seafaring heritage and a desire to plant colonies in Asia, Africa and America. After establishing settlements in Jamestown, Virginia, in 1607 and Plymouth, Massachusetts, in 1620, England was poised to take control of the entire North American coast north of Florida. In 1624, The Netherlands countered by planting a Dutch colony on Manhattan Island, and within a few years, several other settlements were founded on the Hudson River.

Buoyed by the success of settlements along the Hudson River, several Dutch businessmen joined with David Pietersen de Vries to establish a colony near Cape Henlopen. In 1631, while de Vries remained in Holland to gather supplies for the new colony, three dozen Dutch colonists established a settlement near Cape Henlopen on the south side of the entrance to the Delaware Bay. The Dutch settlers lost no time in erecting a wooden stockade on a low bluff opposite the mouth of Lewes Creek. The colonists named their new settlement Swanendael, meaning "Valley of the Swans." Many years later, it became fashionable to call the Dutch settlement Zwaanendael, but that name does not appear in colonial documents. At that time, Dutch

An artist's conception of the Swanendael settlement. *Madelyn Morgan.*

artists such as Rembrandt and Vermeer painted some of Europe's greatest masterpieces. Baruch Spinoza and René Descartes were among Europe's leading thinkers, and Antony van Leeuwenhoek made startling discoveries in science. Banks in the Netherlands handled a major share of Europe's money, and Dutch ships sailed to ports around the world carrying European goods and African slaves. It is possible that there were a few Africans among the Dutch settlers at Zaanenedael, but there is no mention of them in any contemporary documents.

Back in the Netherlands, de Vries received disturbing news that something catastrophic had happened at the new Dutch colony along Lewes Creek. In late 1632, the Dutch entrepreneur set sail for America. When de Vries reached the Delaware Bay, he discovered that the colony had been destroyed, and all the colonists, including any Africans—if there were any—had been killed. The downcast de Vries decided that the Dutch attempt to establish a colony near Cape Henlopen should be abandoned, and after burying the bones of the colonists, he returned to Europe. For the next several decades, there may have been an occasional European who stayed around Lewes Creek for a short time, but there was no organized settlement in the Cape Henlopen area.[19]

The arrival of William Penn, the proprietor of Pennsylvania and Delaware. *Courtesy of the Library of Congress.*

The first African in Delaware for whom there is clear documentation arrived at the other end of the state eight years after the settlement at Swanendael. In 1638, Sweden, aided by Dutch adventurers, established Fort Christina on a tributary of the Delaware River, which is today downtown Wilmington. In 1639, a Swedish ship, fresh from a voyage to the Caribbean, landed an enslaved African named Anthony. For several years, Anthony served on Governor Johan Printz's farm, and he may have been freed by the time that he disappeared from the historical record. There has been speculation that Africans may have been imported into the Swedish settlement, but the record is not conclusive. In 1667, the Dutch and Swedish colonial efforts in America ended when the British defeated the Dutch in the Anglo-Dutch war, and the English took possession of New Netherland.[20] Once the land was in English hands, William Penn eventually became proprietor of both Pennsylvania and Delaware.

CONTRADICTIONS ON REHOBOTH BAY

By the middle of the seventeenth century, the Virginia colony had expanded beyond Jamestown on the west side of the Chesapeake Bay and eastward across the bay to the Delmarva Peninsula. Some of the Virginia colonists migrated northward into Maryland and Delaware. In the second half of the seventeenth century, John Johnson was a second-generation free Black man whose father, Anthony Johnson, may have arrived aboard the *White Lyon* in 1619. John Johnson settled in southern Delaware, where he acquired a substantial tract of four hundred acres on Rehoboth Bay. At that time, the nearest town was Lewes, a small village of a few dozen mostly Dutch colonists who congregated near the failed Zwaanendael settlement.

For the next three decades, John Johnson lived on Rehoboth Bay. He appeared in the Sussex County Courthouse in Lewes to testify in several cases concerning land ownership. In 1704, when Johnson was eighty years old and unable to care for himself, the Sussex County Court ordered that fifty shillings of public money be spent for "keeping and maintaining John Johnson, an old free Negro."[21] The old colonist died sometime after 1707. His burial site is unknown.

The written record of John Johnson contrasts sharply with the archaeological remains of three skeletons recently found at Avery's Rest, a seventeenth-century farm on the banks of Rehoboth Bay. In the 1670s, John Avery, a former Maryland colonist like Johnson, settled on a tract of

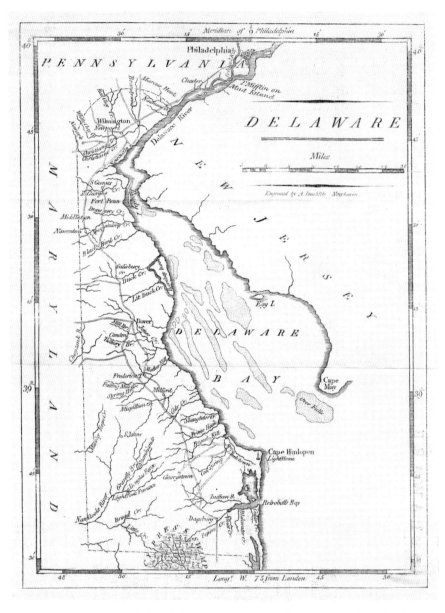

The north–south road paralleling Delaware Bay was an early Underground Railroad route. *Courtesy of the Delaware Public Archives.*

350 acres of land on the north shore of Rehoboth, where he named his new home Avery's Rest. After Avery passed away in 1682, the colonist's house was eventually abandoned and leveled until little remained above ground. In the early twenty-first century, archaeologists digging at Avery's Rest uncovered graves with eleven skeletons that were buried sometime between 1665 and 1695. DNA analysis revealed that eight of the skeletons were of European descent, and three, two adults and one child, were of African heritage. It is assumed that the three people of African heritage who were buried were enslaved by the Avery family. The wear on the bones of all of the adults in both groups indicate that they engaged in hard labor and that everyone at Avery's Rest shared the hard work of maintaining the tobacco plantation on the Mid-Atlantic frontier.

Lacking gravestones and documentary evidence, the archaeologists could not assign names to any of the particular skeletons, but the European skeletons were most likely those of the members of the Avery family. DNA analysis of the bones of the two men and the child in the African group revealed the two adults were of West African heritage, and the child was from East Africa. The location of John Johnson's farm on Rehoboth Bay is not known, but in the sparsely settled Sussex County, it is likely that Johnson came into contact with Avery and his enslaved people. There is abundant archaeological evidence of Avery's Rest and the Black Americans who were held in bondage there, but there is little documentary evidence about the three African people whose remains were found. In colonial Delaware, Black and white, free and enslaved, lived side by side.[22]

A Negro Man Called Black Will

During the late seventeenth century, the free Johnson family may not have been the first Black colonists to arrive in southern Delaware. There were an unknown number of Black and white Delaware colonists who were indentured servants who mortgaged their labor for a set number of years. Indentured servants received no pay for their labor, and they could not move or marry without their master's permission. If an indentured servant ran away from their master and was caught, additional time was added to their years of service. Delaware had a variety of non-free people—apprentices, indentured servants and the enslaved—all of whom were prone to running away. Much of the information about those who left bondage has been gleaned from newspaper advertisements placed by their masters who hoped

RUN away from *Talbot* County-School, on Monday the 5th Day of this Inftant *Auguft*, *George Ewings*, Mafter of the fame School; who took with him a Negro Man named *Nero*, and two Geldings, the one of a grey, the other of a black Colour, the Property of the Vifitors of the fame School. The faid *Ewings* is an *Irifhman*, of a middle Stature, and thin Vifage, is marked with the Small-Pox, and has the Brogue upon his Tongue.

Whoever apprehends the faid *Ewings*, Negro, and Geldings, fo that they may be had again, fhall receive Five Pounds Current Money of *Maryland* as a Reward, paid by the Vifitors of the fame School.

Auguft 7, 1745.   Signed *per* Order,
                                          Wm. GOLDSBOROUGH, Regifter.

Advertisements for runaways included a variety of people. *From the* Maryland Gazette, *August 23, 1745.*

they would be apprehended. There was no newspaper in Delaware until after the American Revolution, but in 1727, the *Maryland Gazette* was founded in Annapolis, Maryland, and it occasionally contained advertisements for fugitives from Maryland's Eastern Shore. In 1728, two white indentured servants ran away from John Austin of Kent County, Maryland, which shared a border with Delaware. Austin advertised in the *Maryland Gazette*: "One is a lusty man, corpulent in body, with short black curled hair, and somewhat grey and bald on the crown; aged about forty….The other is a little man, aged about twenty-four, fresh colour'd, with light brown hair, curling a little at the ends; and walks stooping, and as if one of his legs was shorter than the other." The two servants took with them a variety of carpenter tools and two horses. Austin offered "five pounds for each man, or three pounds for either of the horses."[23]

In 1746, Thomas Woolford of Dorchester County, Maryland, advertised in the *Maryland Gazette*, "Run away from the subscriber, a Negro man, named Liverpool; he is a tall slim fellow, has a very small head and face, long small legs, and had on when he went away a broad cloth coat, a country made Kersey coat, a white shirt, a country linen shirt. He went away the 20th of March, and I am apprehensive he is gone to the northward."[24] Traveling northward from Dorchester County would likely have led the fugitive into Delaware.

The variety of the fugitives was illustrated by this August 23, 1745 *Maryland Gazette* advertisement:

> *Run away from Talbot County School, on Monday 5ᵗʰ day of this instant August, George Ewings, master of the same school, who took with him a negro man named Nero, and two geldings, the one of a grey, the other of a black color, the property of the visitors of the same school. The said Ewings is an Irishman, of a middle stature, and thin visage, is marked with the smallpox, and has the brogue upon his tongue.*[25]

On June 13, 1682, William Clark of Lewes bought a servant named Black Will, and the bill of sale indicated the ambiguous nature of Will's status:

> *Whereas William Clark did buy of Captain John Osborne of Somerset County in the province of Maryland, a Negro man called or known by the name of Black Will for and during his natural life. Nevertheless, the said William Clark do for the encouragement of the aid Negro servant hereby promise, covenant, and agree that if the said Black Will do and shall well and truly serve the said William Clark…Black Will shall be clear and free of and from any further or longer servitude or slavery.*[26]

While it is sometimes noted that Black Will was the first documented enslaved person in Sussex County, the bill of sale made clear that he could gain his freedom after five years of satisfactory service, which would make him more like an indentured servant.

During the years Will served William Clark, the population of the coastal region began to rise, and during the early eighteenth century, the number of enslaved people imported into Sussex County increased dramatically. In 1738, Richard Ellis of Philadelphia directed a typical shipment of enslaved people to land at Lewes. As the ship rode at anchor near Lewes, Jacob Kollock, Ellis's son-in-law, inspected the "merchandise" to ensure they had survived the sea voyage intact. After he had inspected the goods, Kollock ordered that sixteen of the enslaved be taken ashore, and he sold them to residents of Sussex County. At that time, many Philadelphia merchants preferred to import Africans directly into Delaware, which, unlike Pennsylvania, did not have a tariff on the enslaved.[27]

In 1738, Lewes was a small town of several dozen houses that lined two streets that paralleled Lewes Creek. In the middle of town, St. Peter's Episcopal Church sat on four acres of land between Market and Mulberry

Streets, fronting Second Street. The church land was adjacent to the courthouse, authorized in 1681 to be constructed of logs that were at least eight inches thick and topped by "a good strong roof, tight and well-covered." Next to the courthouse stood Philip Russell's tavern at the corner of Second and Mulberry Streets. Russell had once been hauled into court for "suffering persons to play at cards" at his establishment. Russell's tavern eventually passed into the hands of a young merchant named Ryves Holt. The Ryves Holt house is now owned by the Lewes Historical Society.

Except for house servants and the occasional field hand, the number of enslaved people in the Lewes area was relatively small. The arrival of a slave ship at Lewes, however, was not unusual, and the addition of Jacob Kollock's sixteen enslaved people would have caused a significant increase in the town's enslaved population. In all likelihood, Kollock's enslaved people did not remain in Lewes for a long time.

During the early eighteenth century, all thirteen English colonies allowed slavery, and ships carrying the enslaved called on nearly every colonial port. Enterprising European captains loaded their ships with goods and sailed to West Africa, where they traded the merchandise for enslaved people. After the human cargo was stuffed aboard, the ship set sail for the long voyage across the Atlantic Ocean. Upon their arrival in North America, the enslaved were exchanged for lumber, grain, tobacco or other produce. The ship then returned to Europe to complete a three-legged voyage that became known as the Triangular Trade. The middle leg of the triangle that brought the enslaved across the ocean was the infamous Middle Passage, which became synonymous with a journey of unbearable human suffering.[28]

In addition to Pennsylvania, William Penn's colonial holdings included the territory on the western shore of the Delaware Bay. Extending from Cape Henlopen to the border with Pennsylvania, this area was known as the Three Lower Counties on the Delaware and had a degree of autonomy. When Pennsylvania enacted a tariff on the importation of enslaved people, the Three Lower Counties failed to follow suit. Consequently, the enslaved could be imported at Lewes, sold to buyers from Pennsylvania and shipped overland to Philadelphia without paying the tariff. Apparently, this was the reason Kollock's father-in-law, Richard Ellis, a merchant based in Philadelphia, directed Kollock to land the human cargo at Lewes and avoid the tariff. He was not a smuggler, but he took advantage of this legal loophole.[29]

Jints, the only known photograph of an enslaved woman from Delaware. *Courtesy of the Delaware Public Archives.*

Although some of the Africans who landed at Lewes were sent to other colonies, many remained in Sussex County, where they performed a variety of tasks. In *Slavery and Freedom in Delaware*, historian William H. Williams described the chores performed by the enslaved who were owned by Nehemiah Draper of Cedar Creek Hundred: "In addition to clearing, plowing, planting, cultivating, and harvesting corn and wheat, his thirty slaves looked after 105 cattle, 76 sheep, 54 pigs, 20 oxen, 8 horses, and 55 geese. Draper, like many of the era's gentry, was a rural merchant, and his slaves helped in his store and sailed his small sailing vessel up and down inland waterways and the Delaware Bay. In addition, several of his slaves played essential roles in his extensive timbering activities." By the time of the American Revolution, slavery had become an accepted part of the southern Delaware landscape, and the arrival of the first enslaved person in the coastal region had long since been forgotten.[30]

2

LAYING THE FIRST TRACKS

I started and travelled at nights, and lay by in the day time. I went on
northwards, with great fear and anxiety of mind.
—Solomon[31]

Fifty-Dollar Reward

"We hold these truths to be self-evident," wrote Thomas Jefferson in the Declaration of Independence, "that all men are created equal, that they are endowed by their Creator with certain unalienable Rights, that among these are Life, Liberty and the pursuit of Happiness." Despite Jefferson's hypocrisy (he owned several hundred enslaved people and carried on a decades-long liaison with one of his enslaved persons, Sally Hemings, with whom he fathered a number of children who were enslaved the minute they were born), these inspiring words and the American Revolution brought a great number of changes to Delaware and the people in bondage there.[32] Believing that it was "self-evident that all men were created equal," several of the newly independent American states, including Pennsylvania, began to rid themselves of slavery. Founded by William Penn, a prominent member of the Religious Society of Friends (known informally as the Quakers), Pennsylvania and, in particular, the city of Philadelphia, became the northern terminus of the Delaware Underground Railroad. The Quaker belief in equality and pacifism led the religion's strident members to oppose the American Revolution and denounce slavery. Quakers were instrumental in founding the Pennsylvania Abolition Society, the first such group in the United States.[33] Pennsylvania

THOMAS JEFFERSON,

Thomas Jefferson, president, author of the Declaration of Independence and slave owner. *Courtesy of the Library of Congress.*

began the process of gradual abolition when its legislature passed a law that declared anyone born after March 1, 1780, would be free when they turned twenty-eight. Those born before March 1 remained enslaved. Traveling southerners were allowed to bring their enslaved people into nominally free states without fear that they would automatically be set free. Although the enslaved population was small, it was not until the 1840s that the last permanent enslaved resident of the Keystone State died.[34] Neighboring New Jersey followed a similar path of gradual emancipation. It decreed that anyone born after July 4, 1804, would be free when they reached the age of twenty-one for women and twenty-five for men.[35] Ten years after the passage of the law establishing gradual emancipation in Pennsylvania, there were only about three hundred enslaved people in Philadelphia, and the number of people held in perpetual bondage continued to decline as the Black population in the city continued to grow. About eleven thousand people of color, about 10 percent of Philadelphia's total population, lived in in the city in the early nineteenth century. The gradual emancipation process left some Pennsylvania and New Jersey residents enslaved, but the popular sentiment against slavery, however, was such that these two states were considered "free states."

While there were some notable antislavery Delaware residents, such as the Quaker Warner Mifflin, who peppered state legislatures and the United States Congress with letters, petitions and pamphlets advocating the end of slavery, and Methodist Richard Bassett, a delegate to the Constitutional Convention, United States senator and Delaware governor, efforts to enact legislation in Delaware similar to that in Pennsylvania and New Jersey failed.[36] Delaware steadfastly refused to abolish slavery and remained a slave state until the Civil War and the ratification of the Thirteenth Amendment. As slavery slowly disappeared in Pennsylvania and New Jersey, the enslaved in Delaware came to realize that if they escaped to either of those two states, they would be relatively safe from recapture.

While states were beginning to separate into free and slave states, in 1787, the Constitutional Convention met in Philadelphia to devise a new form of

The Constitutional Convention legalized slavery in the United States. *Courtesy of the Library of Congress.*

government for the newly independent United States. During the convention, there was considerable debate about slavery and fugitive freedom seekers, but the words *slave* and *slavery* were not mentioned in the final document. Euphemisms, such as "persons held to service or labor," were used instead. The Constitution required that "No Person held to Service or Labour in one State…escaping into another, shall…be delivered up on claim of the Party to whom such Service or Labour may be due."[37] In essence, the people of a free state would be constitutionally required to capture freedom seekers who had escaped from a slave state, such as Delaware, and return them to those who claimed ownership of them.

At the convention, there was also considerable support for ending the international slave trade, which brought thousands of new enslaved people from Africa each year. And the new Constitution provided that "the Migration or Importation of such Persons as any of the States now existing shall think proper to admit, shall not be prohibited by the Congress prior to the Year one thousand eight hundred and eight."[38] The phrase "such Persons as any of the States now existing shall think proper to admit" referred to the enslaved. While the Constitutional Convention was in session, it is not unreasonable to believe that a few Black freedom seekers from Delaware arrived in Philadelphia and quietly passed by Independence Hall. After the

Constitution was written, the finished document was submitted to the states, and on December 7, 1789, Delaware was the first state to ratify the new form of government, and it earned the nickname "the First State."

Five years after the Constitutional Convention was held in Philadelphia, the flow of freedom seekers from Maryland left many slave owners frustrated. On July 11, 1792, the *Philadelphia National Gazette* reported:

> *Frequent complaints are made in the eastern counties of Maryland of their run-a-way slaves being harboured by certain philanthropic people in the state of Delaware. A gentleman in Maryland who has frequently suffered by desertions of this kind, and has had slaves concealed for years together in the last mentioned state, publicly advertises in the* Delaware Gazette, *that to ease the consciences of those who execrate this kind of property, he will dispose of his slaves to those who will to have them set free, at three fourths of their real value, to be estimated by men of judgment and impartiality.*[39]

The embryonic Delaware Underground Railroad was beginning to take shape.

With the invention of the cotton gin in the 1790s and the expansion of cotton plantations in the Deep South, the demand for enslaved people grew. In Virginia, Maryland and Delaware, however, there was a declining need for enslaved laborers, as these states turned from tobacco to wheat, corn and other crops that were less labor intensive. Slave owners soon discovered that raising enslaved people as a "cash crop" could be profitable. In addition, the enslaved in those three states now labored under the real threat that they could be sold to the Deep South, where conditions for the enslaved were more brutal and escape was more difficult. In Delaware, freedom seekers became more determined than ever to reach Pennsylvania.

In 1785, Delaware's first successful newspaper, the *Delaware Gazette*, began publication in Wilmington. It printed advertisements for people escaping bondage and fleeing from or through the First State. Like the advertisements carried by the *Maryland Gazette*, the *Delaware Gazette*'s advertisements featured physical descriptions of runaways and included descriptions of the clothes they wore. The advertisements differed in that those in the early nineteenth-century *Delaware Gazette* prominently headlined the substantial reward offered for fugitives. The October 11, 1809 edition of the *Delaware Gazette* carried an advertisement for a runaway named Philp Brown, whose owner offered a $150 reward, and an advertisement that promised "50 Dollars Reward" for the capture of a Black man named Israel, a runaway from a camp meeting in Worcester County, Maryland. The fact that the person who claimed ownership of Israel advertised in the Wilmington, Delaware newspaper and offered $50 if the fugitive was taken out of state and only $15 if he were taken in Maryland suggested that Israel had gone northward through Delaware.[40]

In the early nineteenth century, camp meetings were a new religious phenomenon that became a permanent part of the Delaware landscape. Part of the religious revival movement, camp meetings were held outdoors, with attendees living in tents for about a week. According to William Morgan, a longtime Delaware resident and Methodist preacher, the first camp meeting on the Delmarva Peninsula was held in 1805 in Kent County, Delaware, near Smyrna at a small creek known appropriately as Chapel Branch.[41] The camp meetings were well organized, with the campgrounds laid out in military precise rectangles fronting a pulpit for the preachers and a section reserved for Black Americans.[42] The camp meetings and other church services provided a chance for Black residents, both free and enslaved, from different locations to come together and socialize. These services were an opportunity for the enslaved to learn about which towns and farms they should avoid and which places were friendly to freedom seekers. They learned that Quakers might be friendly, and they learned how to identity them with their broadbrim hats, long coats and speech (they were to address them as "thee" and "thou" instead of "you"). Camp meetings also provided Black Americans who were contemplating running away with a chance to learn about the North Star, how to locate it and how to follow it. These gatherings also gave Black Americans a forum in which to share tips with potential runaways, such as rubbing cow dung on their shoes if they had them or on their bare feet if they did not have

50 Dollars Reward.

RAN away from the Camp Meeting, in in Worcester County, on Monday the twenty-eighth of August last, a NEGRO MAN named ISRAEL, upwards of thirty years of age, about six feet high, with a very bright yellow complexion, the property of Miss Polly Elzey of Somerset county, and hired the present year by the subscriber to James Furnip, of Somerset. Any person who will take up said Negro and secure him so that the owner gets him again, shall, if taken out of the state, receive the above reward, and if taken in the state, and out of the county, Twenty-Five dollars—and if taken in the county, Fifteen dollars, to be paid by

Robert Elzey.

Somerset County, Princess Ann,
September 12, 1809. 9t.

One Hundred and Fifty Dollars Reward.

RAN away from the subscriber, living in Somerset county, state of Maryland, a negro fellow named PHILIP BROWN, about five feet eight or nine inches high; a little knock kneed, a blacksmith by trade, has a yellowish complexion, and is a handy sensible fellow at any business; had on when he went away a country made over jacket, striped with red and black; a pair of country made long trowsers, dyed a dark colour, old hat, shoes, and tow linen shirt. Whoever takes up the said negro and brings him to me shall have the above reward if taken out of the state of Maryland.
LAMBERT HYLAND.
September 5. 4w

Cash rewards were offered for the return of fugitives. *From the* Delaware Gazette, *October 11, 1809.*

At camp meetings, freedom seekers exchanged information about the Delaware Underground Railroad. *Courtesy of the Library of Congress.*

shoes—this was done to smother their scent and confuse the dogs that the slave catchers used to track fugitives.

The federal constitutional requirement that enslaved people fleeing their masters from one state to another be returned was reinforced by the passage of the Fugitive Slave Law of 1793, which required state governments to assist in capturing and returning freedom seekers to those who claimed ownership of them.[43] Although it gave slave catchers legal standing, the law proved ineffective. Despite the 1793 Fugitive Slave Law and the complaints of Maryland slave owners, the Underground Railroad continued to evolve and made a substantial step forward when Solomon Bayley ran away from his owner. Bayley was born in Delaware around the time of the American Revolution. His grandmother was born in Africa, and when she was about eleven years old, she was taken to America and sold into slavery in Virginia. According to Bayley, "My grandmother was bought into of the most barbarous families of that day; and although treated hard, was said to have fifteen sons and daughters: she lived to a great age, until she appeared weary of life."[44] Bayley's mother was taken to Delaware, where she also had a large family of thirteen children. As Solomon explained, his brothers and sister "were all sold and scattered wide apart, some to the east, and some west, north, and south."[45] Solomon was sold to an owner in Accomack County, Virginia, and then taken to Richmond, where he ran away from his owners and made his way back across the Chesapeake to Virginia's Eastern Shore. Bayley made his way through Maryland to Sussex County, Delaware, where he was one of the earliest travelers on what became the Delaware Underground Railroad. Walking northward along the King's Highway east of the Great Cypress Swamp through Dagsboro, Milton, Milford and to

The Camden Meeting House was a suspected station on the Delaware Underground Railroad. *Courtesy of the Delaware Public Archives.*

Camden, Bayley avoided the slave catchers and others who would return him to his former master by employing the practices that future freedom seekers would adopt on their journeys through Delaware.[46] According to Bayley, "I started and traveled at nights, and lay by in the daytime. I went on northwards, with great fear and anxiety of mind. It abode on my mind that I should meet with some difficulty before I got to Dover; however, I tried to study on the promises of the Almighty." Bayley traveled on until he reached Anderson's Crossroads, south of Milford at the intersection of what is now Delaware Route 30, also known as Cedar Creek Road, Benson Road and Neal Road.

Bayley was helped by the fact that he had lived in Delaware for several years and was familiar with many of the roads, but after he reached Anderson's Crossroads, the fugitive lost his bearings, and he had to ask a stranger for directions to Camden. As so often happened, the stranger decided to turn Bayley over to the authorities, but after a long chase through the woods, Bayley was able to elude the stranger. His success was short-lived.[47]

On July 24, 1799, Bayley reached Camden, where he was confronted by his owner, who threatened to take him back to Virginia. Bayley, however, argued that the Delaware law made him a free man. After he was taken to Virginia, he intended to file suit in Dover for his freedom. According to Bayley, after some discussion, "He sold me my time for eighty dollars, and I dropped the lawsuit. I went to work and worked it out in a shorter time than he gave me, and then I was free from man."[48] Like the more famous trailblazers of the American West, Solomon Bayley pioneered a route that would become the backbone of the Delaware Underground Railroad. From 1799 until the start of the Civil War, hundreds of fugitive enslaved people followed in Solomon Bayley's footsteps as they made their journeys to freedom.

For Their Good Service

Solomon Bayley's purchase of his freedom would have been rare in the Deep South, where dozens—if not hundreds—of enslaved people were held in bondage on a single plantation and their opportunity to earn money for their work was virtually nonexistent. In Delaware, slave holders rarely owned more than a dozen enslaved people. Some enslaved people acquired skills that enabled them to take on outside work, earn money and buy their freedom. In the late eighteenth and early nineteenth centuries, there were a number of ironworks that mined the bog iron found in the low-lying ground around the Nanticoke and Indian Rivers and their tributaries.[49] Ironmaking was a labor-intensive process that required men with strong backs and steady determination. The bog ore needed to be wrestled from the ground and carted across the primitive roads of southern Delaware to a furnace, where charcoal provided the heat needed to smelt the raw ore into pig iron. The pig iron was then taken to a forge, where it was fashioned into finished products.[50]

The ironworks of Delaware required a large number of blacksmiths, forgemen, colliers and other skilled workers. Several of the southern Delaware forges and furnaces used a mixed labor force of white and Black workers, some of whom were enslaved, who were trained in several skilled occupations. Because a skilled worker was costly to replace, many owners gave their skilled enslaved people better housing, food and other privileges that were denied most field hands. Some skilled enslaved people were allowed to take on outside work, and they were permitted to keep some of the money they generated from this extra labor. A number of skilled enslaved people were able to save enough money from these extra assignments to buy their own freedom.

Such was the case of blacksmith Benjamin Johnstone. "I was born a slave," said Johnstone to begin his account of the trials and tribulations of his remarkable life.[51] Born in Sussex County, Delaware, several years before the start of the American Revolution, Johnstone was shuttled from owner to owner for most of his life, but along the way, Johnstone learned blacksmithing skills and became a dedicated, hard worker. One day, Johnstone noticed a suspicious man approaching his owner, who was concentrating on hammering out a piece of iron. Johnstone recalled, "I saw the fellow put his hand behind and grasp a very long knife; at the same time, he swore he would instantly kill my master." Johnstone grabbed the man and wrestled the knife away. His owner was so appreciative of Johnstone for saving his life that the two men agreed that if Johnstone could raise enough money to compensate his owner for the loss of his valuable enslaved laborer, Johnstone would be freed.[52]

Johnstone's arrangement with his owner was not without its perils. Given time off to raise the money to buy his way out of slavery, Johnstone went to Baltimore, where there was a high demand for his blacksmithing skills. Unfortunately, he was arrested as a runaway and thrown into jail. His owner secured Johnstone's release, and Johnstone returned to Delaware, where he was barely able to avoid being kidnapped and taken to Georgia. By this time, Johnstone was fed up with the hazards of living in a slave state, and he fled to New Jersey.

Johnstone settled in Woodbury, New Jersey, changed his first name from Benjamin to Abraham and was married. Johnstone, however, continued his rough-and-tumble ways. In 1797, the Delaware native was accused of murder, found guilty and sentenced to death. Before his execution, Johnstone composed a summary of his life and a poignant letter to his wife that closed with, "I've kissed this paper and…I bid you, my dear wife, not the farewell of a day, month, nor year, but an eternal farewell."[53]

As was the case with the ill-fated Benjamin Johnstone, some Delaware owners recognized that their enslaved people should be rewarded for the years of unpaid labor. In 1786, an enslaved family—Adam, Rebecca and their daughter, Mintee—was freed because of "their good service."[54] On November 11, 1812, a Sussex County lawyer wrote, "Know all men by these present, that I, Outerbridge Horsey, have manumitted, set free, and forever discharged…from my service…after the expiration of the terms of service herein stated, the Negroes [listed below]." This set a schedule—from as little as five years to as long as thirty years—for the release of these enslaved people from bondage. Horsey provided a path to freedom to fourteen slaves.[55]

Manumission papers. *Courtesy of the Delaware Public Archives.*

At the beginning of the American Revolution, in 1775, 95 percent of Delaware's Black population was enslaved, but by manumissions for "good service," the enslaved purchasing their own freedom and other reasons, that percentage rapidly declined. By 1790, 70 percent of Black people in Delaware were enslaved, and by 1810, only 24 percent of Black people in Delaware were held in bondage.[56] That percentage continued to decline until 1860 and the start of the Civil War, when only 8 percent of the Black population in Delaware was enslaved.[57] The increased number of free Black people in Delaware increased the chances of success for those fugitives fleeing on the First State's developing Underground Railroad. Although Delaware's residents were intimidated by the threat of reprisals and were sometimes swayed by the reward offered for runaways, Delaware's free Black population could by a wink and a nod and a silent shake of the head indicate the road to be taken and warn of the presence of unfriendly residents. Delaware's free Black residents were also known to tear down the wanted posters placed along the likely routes fugitives took.

STEEL FLEES AGAIN

After Sidney Steel's abortive attempt to escape with her four children to New Jersey, her owner punished her by locking her in a garret every night. After several months, her owner decided that she had been cured of her desire for freedom. He was wrong. Shortly after she was released and allowed to move about the farm, she began plotting her escape to rejoin her husband in New Jersey. Now a veteran on Delaware's Underground Railroad, she better appreciated the difficulties of traveling with four children and the attention they brought. She believed that if she took only two of the children, she would have a better chance of reaching New Jersey and reuniting with Levin. The girls would face not only a life of hard labor and physical punishment but also possible sexual abuse if they remained. For Sidney, the heart-wrenching question became which of her children she would take with her and which ones she would leave behind. The boys were a few years old, and they were entering their valuable years as enslaved laborers, and Sidney may have believed that their owner would treat them well. In addition, their grandmother was still on their owner's farm to look after them. It was a decision that no mother should have to make, but Sidney's calculations made sense, and one night in the early winter of 1805—without telling the boys, so they could not inadvertently betray her plans—she took her two girls and again began the trek across Delaware to New Jersey.[58]

In all likelihood, Sidney followed the same route from Caroline County to Greenwich, New Jersey, that she took on her first escape. She knew what roads to follow, what houses to avoid and which people were friendly. It appears that Sidney and Levin established a rendezvous point where they would meet before they reached New Jersey. If so, she probably traveled eastward across Delaware to Pearson's Cove, where Levin would have crossed the Delaware River to meet her. At one point, carrying the two young girls so fatigued Sidney that she could not continue. Should she stop and seek shelter until she was rested and could move on? Was the rendezvous point with Levin in sight? It appears that Sidney and the girls were close to meeting up with Levin. She bundled up one of the girls and left her alongside the road as she hurried to meet Levin, who rushed back to retrieve the infant. Once they crossed the Delaware River into New Jersey, Levin, Sidney and the two girls moved from Greenwich to Indian Mills, about two dozen miles away, where they felt safer from the slave catchers. Levin and Sidney plotted ways to rescue their two boys from Maryland, but it was too late. When their former owner found that Sidney had fled with the girls, he sold the boys to a slave trader who took them to Kentucky.[59]

THOMAS GARRETT AND THE DEVIL ON THE NANTICOKE

Thomas Garrett was the quintessential Quaker who became a fearless stationmaster on the Delaware Underground Railroad. Garrett's great-grandfather arrived in Pennsylvania two years after William Penn established his colony. Through the years, the Garrett family never lost their Quaker fervor for the equality of all people and disdain for slavery. The future abolitionist was born in 1789 on the family's homestead in Upper Darby, Pennsylvania, on the western edge of Philadelphia. Thomas, one of thirteen children, was raised on the family farm, where he assisted his parents and twelve siblings with the endless chores associated with working the surrounding acreage. Garrett's father was also a skilled blacksmith who made some of the iron tools needed on the farm, and through him, young Thomas learned ironworking skills.[60]

Thomas Garrett, a Wilmington stationmaster on the Delaware Underground Railroad. *From Still, Underground Rail Road.*

One day in 1813, when Thomas was twenty-four years old, he returned home from working in the fields to find the rest of the family distraught. One of the family's free Black household servants had been seized by a suspected slave trader, placed in a horse-drawn wagon and driven off. Thomas did not hesitate; he mounted a horse and went in hot pursuit of the kidnappers, whose wagon had a damaged wheel that left a distinctive track that was easy to follow. Garrett chased the culprits into Philadelphia, near the Delaware River, and then northward to Kensington, where Garrett was able to snatch the servant from the kidnappers and return her to the Garrett home. This incident was an epiphany for Garrett. According to a biography written at the time of his death, "During this ride, he afterwards assured his friends he felt the iniquity and abomination of the whole system of slavery borne in upon his mind so strongly as to fairly appall him, and he seemed to hear a voice within him, assuring him that his work in life must be to help and defend this persecuted race."[61] After this epiphany, Garrett vowed to assist any freedom seekers he encountered, and his Wilmington house and business became known as "refuges for fugitives."[62] The kidnapping incident taught Garrett the frailty of the freedom of any Black person, as they could, at any time, be taken away and subjected to a lifetime of forced labor. It was a lesson that burned in Garrett's soul and motivated much of his future life. Five years after rescuing his family's housemaid, he joined the Pennsylvania Anti-Slavery Society. The abolition of slavery and the assisting of freedom seekers become Garrett's lifetime work. Four years later, in 1822, Garrett, now thirty-three years old, left his family's homestead and moved to Wilmington, Delaware, where he established a successful hardware store.[63]

If Thomas Garrett was the prototypical Quaker, abolitionist and friend to all people, Patty Cannon was the model godless murderer, kidnapper and enemy to all. Cannon's ancestorial roots are cloudy. In the late eighteenth century, she married Jesse Cannon, a member of the family who operated Cannon's Ferry across the Nanticoke River. The ferry was an important link in the early southern Delaware transportation network. It still operates today under the name Woodland Ferry. By the early years of the nineteenth century, Patty Cannon had started her life of crime in southern Delaware. From her home in Sussex County, on the border between Delaware and Maryland, she commanded a gang of cutthroats led by her son-in-law, Joe Johnson. In 1813, when Garrett had his epiphany on the road to Philadelphia, Patty Cannon engineered the murder of a slave trader who had been foolish enough to tell her he was carrying a large sum of cash.[64] By the time Garrett had moved to Wilmington and established himself as a friend to all Black Americans, Patty was kidnapping free Black people and selling them to slave traders. According to the abolitionist Jesse Torrey, who investigated the kidnappings in southern Delaware, the kidnapping gangs were like "beasts of prey...extending their ravages, generally attended with bloodshed and sometimes murder, and spreading terror and consternation amongst both freemen and slaves throughout the sandy regions form the western to the eastern shores. These 'two-legged featherless animals' or human blood-hounds, when overtaken (rarely) by messengers of the law, are generally found armed with instruments of death, sometimes with pistols with latent spring daggers attached to them!"[65]

A kidnapping expedition to Philadelphia by Cannon's henchmen netted five Black people, who were then taken to southern Delaware. The five Philadelphia captives were joined by Mary Fisher, a kidnapping victim from Delaware. The Cannon gang loaded aboard a sloop in the Nanticoke River, and they set sail for the South. After a week at sea, the sloop landed in southern Alabama, where the kidnap victims began a grueling march northward across the state. The shoeless prisoners were forced to march about thirty miles each day, and when they complained of sore feet and being unable to keep up the pace, the prisoners were flogged, sometimes receiving more than fifty lashes. At Tuscaloosa, one of the kidnapped victims was sold to a slave trader. Another was able to slip away but was recaptured and flogged with a handsaw. After one severe beating, the wife of one of the kidnappers remarked, "It did her good to see him beat the boys."[66]

Finally, the march ended seven miles west of Rocky Springs, Mississippi, where most of the surviving captives were sold to John W. Hamilton, a plantation owner. To verify his ownership of these Black people, Hamilton was given a fictitious bill of sale that was fabricated by one of the gang members; it indicated that the kidnapped victims were enslaved people. Hamilton looked at the bill of sale, and he sensed that something was wrong. When Hamilton was able to be alone with the kidnapping victims, they told him they were free. It took a great deal of courage for them to admit this to Hamilton. Kidnap victims were told that if they claimed to be free, they would be severely beaten.[67] After Solomon Northup, a free Black man who had been kidnapped into slavery, tried to explain that he was a free man, he was so severely battered that he wrote in his account of being kidnapped into bondage, *Twelve Years a Slave*, he was determined "to say nothing further on the subject of my having been born a freeman. It would but expose me to mal-treatment, and diminish the chances of liberation." At the moment of his liberation, Northup recalled, "For ten years, I had dwelt among them [the other slaves], in the field and in the cabin, borne the same hardships, partaken the same fare, mingled my griefs with theirs, participated in the same scanty joys; nevertheless, not until this hour, the last I was to remain among them, had the remotest suspicion of my true name, or the slightest knowledge of my real history, been entertained by any one of them."[68]

Hamilton was convinced, however, that these captives were telling the truth, and he called his lawyer. The two drafted a detailed letter to Joseph Watson, the mayor of Philadelphia. Born in 1764, Watson was a carpenter and lumber merchant who was first elected as an alderman in 1822. Two years later, the city council elected him to be mayor, a post he held for four years. When Watson received Hamilton's letter, he turned it over to the newspapers, which caught the attention of the Wilmington Quaker Thomas Garrett. The horrors that Mary Fisher experienced exemplified

Free Black Americans were routinely kidnapped in southern Delaware. *From Torrey,* A Portraiture of Slavery.

the treatment Garrett envisioned when his household maid was kidnapped from his family farm in Upper Darby, Pennsylvania. Garrett wrote to Mayor Watson, "I find by our papers that thou hast received a communication from the state of Mississippi respecting several colour'd persons, said to be kidnapped, one of which is stated to have lived in this place [Wilmington]. There is a female of the name Charity Fisher that left this place the 6th day of the 10th month, expecting to return in a few days that has not since been heard of by her friends. Every circumstance except the first name would induce me to believe it was the same."

Mayor Watson assigned a constable to go to Mississippi with orders to retrieve the kidnapping victims. The constable's mission was successful, and he was able to transport them back to their homes. Mary Fisher was afraid to return to Pennsylvania by sea. She decided to wait at Hamilton's plantation, where she was treated as a free person, until she could travel by land. According to the abolitionist newspaper *American Watchman and Delaware Advertiser*:

> *The rescue of these poor creatures is a subject of rejoicing for all benevolent persons and is chiefly due to the indefatigable and charitable zeal of Mr. Watson, the Mayor. Too much credit cannot be given to the excellent dispositions and intelligent vigilance, with which he pursued that*

interesting object. It is but justice to add that he was earnestly seconded by many exemplary citizens in Mississippi, Alabama and other places.... [I]t is certain that there are gangs of kidnappers incessantly prowling for prey and against whom constant watchfulness should be practiced and recommended.[69]

Watson was determined to destroy Patty Cannon's gang and "the mazes of this infernal plot, by which a great number of free-born children, during several years past, have been seduced away...by a gang of desperadoes, whose haunts and headquarters are known to have been on the dividing line between the states of Delaware and Maryland, low down on the peninsula, between the Delaware and Chesapeake Bays."[70]

In 1827, Watson offered a $500 reward "for the apprehension and prosecution to conviction of any person concerned in the forcible abduction of the free colored persons from the city of Philadelphia." The mayor waited to see if the reward offer would produce enough evidence to arrest Patty Cannon or any members of her gang.[71] In April 1829, Patty's tenant farmer was plowing a field near her house when he began to tackle a low-lying spot that had been covered with brush for several years. As the horse trod into the dip in the field, the farmer was startled to see the animal sink into the ground up to its haunches. After the farmer extricated his horse from the ground, he dug through the dirt to see why the ground was so soft. It took only a few minutes of digging before he discovered human bones. The tenant farmer rushed to tell others what he had found, and soon, a crowd assembled, including one of Cannon's gang members, who told how Patty killed several people and buried them in the yard. Patty was arrested and indicted for murder. According to the *Baltimore Niles Register*, "This woman is now between 60 and 70 years of age and looks more like a man than a woman; but old as she is, she is believed to be heedless and heartless as the most abandoned wretch that breathes."[72]

It appeared that southern Delaware would host a sensational trial at the old wooden courthouse in Georgetown, but on May 23, 1829, the *Niles Register* reported, "Patty Cannon died in jail on the 11th instant."[73] The cause of her death was unknown and remains a mystery.

There is no doubt that Patty Cannon intercepted freedom seekers on Delaware's Underground Railroad. A few weeks after her death, the Wilmington newspaper the *Delaware Register* published an account of the Cannon gang posing as agents on the Underground Railroad. According to the newspaper, the gang included several Black men who would lure fugitives into a trap so that the kidnappers could capture them. One of these Black men was particularly adept at posing as a friend who would connect the freedom seekers to agents of the Underground Railroad. According to the *Delaware Register*, "This individual, upon one occasion, prevailed upon a man who was slave to a person in Worcester County, Md., had a free wife and seven male children, between the ages of 6 and 18 years, to accompany him to Camden, in this state, with the assurances that he would be able to procure a pass from the members of the Friends Society in that place, with which he would be enabled to pass into the state of New Jersey and escape from the service of his master."[74] The turncoat led this father to Patty Cannon's house, where he was given a document with a large seal on it that was supposed to be his pass to New Jersey. The turncoat then told the freedom seeker to go back to fetch his family so that they could accompany him to freedom. According to the *Delaware Register*, the fugitive "immediately went back to his wife and children, telling them a fine tale of the favorable situation their husband and father had procured, induced them to follow him, who were also conveyed into the same trap [at Patty Cannon's house], and the next morning after their arrival, they were all shipped off, never more to be heard of by their relations or friends."[75]

In the 1820s, when Patty Cannon's gang's activities kidnapping free people of color from Philadelphia, Baltimore and southern Delawarewere at their height, the Underground Railroad began to blossom. The fugitives who were fleeing their owners learned that the area around the Nanticoke River was a place to be avoided, and the main route to freedom—the route pioneered by Solomon Bayley—lay on the other side of the Great Cypress Swamp.

MONUMENT TO A MISTAKE

Nothing drove fear into the hearts of slave owners more than the prospect of a slave revolt. In colonial America, there were several occasions when slave owners suspected that those they held in bondage were planning an uprising. In 1741 New York City, which had the largest enslaved population outside of Charleston, South Carolina, there were several mysterious fires that were blamed on the city's poor white and Black population. Believing that there was a plot to burn the city down, the authorities arrested scores of suspected conspirers and executed thirty-three people, mostly Black, who were either burned at the stake or hanged.[76] In 1800, plans of a rebellion in Virginia by Gabriel Prosser were uncovered and quashed, and two dozen people were

Nat Turner's rebellion caused a wave of fear across Delaware. *Courtesy of the Library of Congress.*

hanged as a result. Denmark Vesey's alleged revolt in South Carolina was likewise discovered before it was put into action, and over thirty people were executed.[77] The most chilling slave revolt was led by Nat Turner in Virginia. In 1831, Turner used a hatchet to brutally hack his owner to death, and then he led an insurrection of enslaved people in Virginia that left over fifty people dead.

Turner's bloody rampage sent shivers down the spines of the residents of Maryland, Delaware and other slave states. In the area near the Nanticoke River, rumors spread that bands of runaway enslaved people were gathering in the Great Cypress Swamp, and a band of hooligans decided to play a prank. On Election Day 1831, the pranksters assembled on the banks of the Nanticoke River within sight of the town of Seaford. They divided into two groups, one of which brandished firearms. The group with guns lagged behind the others, who started running toward the town. The other jokers pretended to fire on the others, some of whom fell to the ground, pretending to be shot, and others ran into the Seaford, spreading the news that a band of Black people had landed a short distance from Seaford and killed several white men. The marauding band of Americans was said to be marching on Seaford, bent on causing havoc and destruction.[78]

The practical joke fed the latent fears of the white population of Delaware and created a panic. Some residents fled to the forest to hide until the marauders passed. Others took up arms to confront the supposed band of desperados in deadly combat. The news of the alleged uprising, now estimated at 1,500 armed Black people marching along the banks of the Nanticoke River, spread across Delaware. Many communities attempted to disarm all people of color, free or enslaved, and towns prepared for war as if they were meeting an army of foreign invaders.[79]

Unlike Patty Cannon's real kidnapping of scores of Black people that caused barely a ripple in Delaware, the practical joke resulted in the passage of a series of repressive laws aimed at curbing the activities of free Black people. These laws made it illegal for free Black residents to own firearms or hold religious meetings. Although church services provided an opportunity for Black residents to exchange information about the Underground Railroad, many white residents believed, without any evidence, that the Black churches were fomenting rebellion. Henceforth, religious services could be held only under the supervision of "respectable white persons." In addition, out-of-state Black preachers, who were suspected of bringing plans of insurrection to Delaware, were banned. Violators were subject to be sold into slavery.[80]

The Black residents of Sussex County had a few years to adjust to these Draconian laws, when William Yates, an agent for the American Anti-Slavery Society, arrived in Delaware to observe the conditions of people of color. Yates found that the laws passed after Nat Turner's Rebellion were designed to reduce the power and influence of people of color. In addition, the Delaware law that made it illegal to sell enslaved people to out-of-state buyers was being ignored. These added restrictions on people of color placed Black Americans further away from the normal protections of the law and helped convince more freedom seekers to board the Underground Railroad.

3

DELAWARE'S UNDERGROUND RAILROAD STARTS ROLLING

With us, it was a doubtful liberty at most and almost certain death if we failed.
For my part, I would prefer death to hopeless bondage.
—Frederick Douglass[81]

BIRTH OF DELAWARE'S UNDERGROUND RAILROAD

By the second decade of the nineteenth century, fueled by the westward movement of settlers, the United States had grown to comprise twenty-two states. Exactly half of these states were considered free states, and the other half were slave states. When Missouri was ready to be admitted to the nation as a slave state, there was no apparent free territory that was ready to be admitted as a free state to preserve the balance of free and slave states. With the immense territory of the Louisiana Purchase rapidly being settled and new states being admitted, this question of the balance between free and slave was bound to come up in the ensuing years. In 1820, a compromise was struck that promised to solve the problem for years to come. Missouri was admitted as a slave state, and to preserve the balance between free and slave states, Maine was sliced off from Massachusetts and admitted as a free state. Furthermore, a line was drawn at 36°30' through the Louisiana Purchase. The area north of that line would be free territory, and the area south of it would be open to slavery. The Missouri Compromise, or as it is sometimes known, the Compromise of 1820, divided the country into free and slave states. In the Deep South, the free states were hundreds of miles away, and potential fugitives faced overwhelming obstacles in their attempts to achieve freedom. In the upper South, nearby free states provided potential runaways with a closer destination, and most successful fugitives came from Kentucky, Virginia, Maryland and Delaware.[82] The western routes of the Underground Railroad ran through Kentucky into Ohio and eventually Canada. In the east, fugitives' primary destination was Philadelphia, and many fugitives followed routes—by land and by water—through Delaware to the Pennsylvania city.

Whatever branch fugitives followed, they had to avoid the slave catchers and their hunting dogs. Fugitives also needed to be wary of the regular patrols that roamed bridges, crossroads and other likely checkpoints on their way north. Freedom seekers had the North Star to guide them toward the free states, but they had no maps to estimate where they were, the specific roads to take and how long the trip would take. According to Douglass, "To look at the map and observe the proximity of Eastern Shore, Maryland, to Delaware and Pennsylvania, it may seem to the reader quite absurd to regard the proposed escape as a formidable undertaking.…The real distance was great enough, but the imagined distance was, to our ignorance, much greater."[83]

In southern Delaware, those fugitives who left Dorchester and Caroline Counties in Maryland also ran the risk of encountering Patty Cannon's gang of kidnappers. There were, however, pockets of help, including in the home of Levin Thompson. One of the richest people in Sussex County, Thompson was a free Black man who moved from Dorchester County, Maryland, to Sussex County, Delaware, toward the end of the eighteenth century, when Cannon's gang was active. Thompson owned several hundred acres of farmland and operated a gristmill and a sawmill. He also organized a small textile business, which produced two thousand yards of cloth a year. To operate his extensive holdings, Thompson employed numerous free Black people, and many of his workers purchased the freedom of their relatives. The prosperous entrepreneur also served as an informal banker for his neighbors, both Black and white.[84]

For some of his enterprises, Thompson formed partnerships with his white neighbors, who were able to assist him through the tangled legal network that restricted Black people.[85] Thompson was known to have assisted kidnapped Black Americans, and although there is no direct documentation that says Thompson's farm was a stop on the embryonic Underground Railroad, it is difficult to believe that he did not assist fugitives who showed up on his doorstep.

Levin Thompson's enterprises were located west of the Great Cypress Swamp that straddled the Delaware-Maryland border. Historian Francis Vincent wrote in 1870, "At the southern border of the state is a great morass called the Cypress Swamp, about twelve miles in length.…It contains a great variety of trees and plants, mostly cypress trees (called by the residents cedars) and an immense quantity of huckleberry bushes and is infested with wild animals." Among the wild animals that made the swamp their home were deer, bears, a variety of birds and a number of snakes.[86]

In the early decades of the nineteenth century, a sizable free Black population developed in southern Delaware, fueled by manumissions from the ironworks in the vicinity of the Great Cypress Swamp. In addition to its potentially friendly residents, the swamp offered excellent places for fugitives to hide. In some of the heavily wooded areas and swamps of the South, fugitives took up permanent residences and sometimes banded together to defend these runaway communities, sometimes called maroons. Some of these southern maroons boasted a population of several hundred residents, and the fugitive community in the Great Dismal Swamp on the border between North Carolina and Virginia contained several hundred people.[87] There is no evidence of a maroon of any size being formed in Delaware's Great Cypress Swamp. It is more likely that fugitives used the swamp for what was known as "lying out," the practice of running away with no clear destination in mind and remaining away until they were tired of fending off the snakes, insects and other wildlife and returned to the owner's farm. Eventually, a route on the northern edge of swamp became popular with freedom seekers.

THOMAS GARRETT, STATIONMASTER

Thomas Garrett's involvement in the rescue of Mary Fisher was just one instance in which the Quaker businessman became known as a friend of Wilmington's Black population. In August 1826, Garrett was appointed the administrator of the estate of Charles Bohonon, a free Black resident of Wilmington.[88] In December, Garrett chaired a meeting of the Society for the Encouragement of Free Labor held at Wilmington Town Hall.[89] The society, made up of Quakers, abolitionists and free Black people, advocated for the boycott of goods produced by enslaved labor. By the 1830s, Garrett had garnered a reputation for assisting fugitives on the Underground Railroad, and he had established himself as a leading voice for the abolitionist movement in Delaware. Most of the Underground Railroad stationmasters and agents in Delaware operated in secret. In 1845, Frederick Douglass noted:

> *I have never approved of the very public manner in which some of our western friends have conducted what they call the Underground Railroad. I honor those good men and women for their noble daring and applaud them for willingly subjecting themselves to bloody persecution by openly avowing their participation in the escape of slaves. I, however, can see very little good resulting from such a course, either to themselves or the slaves escaping; while upon the other hand, I see and feel assured that those open declarations are positive evil to the slaves remaining, who are seeking to escape. They do nothing towards enlightening the slave, whilst they do much towards enlightening the master. They stimulate him to greater watchfulness and enhance his power to capture his slave. We owe something to the slave south of the line as well as to those north of it; and in aiding the latter on their way to freedom, we should be careful to do nothing which would be likely to hinder the former from escaping from slavery.*[90]

Unlike most eastern stationmasters, Garrett was not shy about letting others know what he was doing. He recruited a cadre of Black and white residents to assist him in transporting fugitives through Wilmington to Philadelphia and other communities in Pennsylvania. Garrett kept a tally of the fugitives he assisted, and hardly a week went by in which a freedom seeker didn't stop at his Wilmington home or his hardware store looking for assistance. As the Delaware route of the Underground Railroad became more popular, the slave catchers learned to keep a lookout for fugitives leaving Wilmington and heading north. One of the places that was carefully watched was the bridge over the Brandywine River that led out of Wilmington. One time, a fugitive named Bob wanted to go to Philadelphia via the bridge. Garrett advised him not to go that way, since the bridge was carefully patrolled. Bob insisted, and Garrett sent one of his helpers to escort him to the bridge. Sure enough, when the freedom seeker attempted to cross the bridge, he was apprehended as a suspected fugitive by a constable. Not knowing for sure that the man was free or enslaved, the constable took him to a magistrate to decide the issue.

When Garrett learned about this, he immediately went to the office where Bob was being held. By this time, news had spread about the man's capture, and a crowd had gathered. Pushing his way to the doorway, the Wilmington Quaker knocked loudly at the door to the magistrate's office. The door was

WILMINGTON, DEL.   Friends Meeting House, 4th and West Sts.

Mrs Chapman

2646

The Friends Meeting House attended by Thomas Garrett. *Courtesy of the Delaware Public Archives.*

opened, and Garrett entered the room, where someone demanded to know who he was. The businessman announced, "Thomas Garrett!" When Garrett saw the man who had been escorted to the bridge, he asked innocently, "Why, Bob, why is thee here for?" Bob replied that he was arrested as a fugitive enslaved man. Garrett knew full well that Bob was enslaved, and his Quaker scruples would not allow him to lie. Garrett scoffed, "A slave? Bob, thee must come with me." All those present assumed that Garrett knew the man and that he was free. The Quaker, who had maintained the letter of truth, and the freedom seeker left the magistrate's office. Later, Garrett directed Bob to take another route to Philadelphia. This time, he followed Garrett's advice and took a different route out of Wilmington.[91]

Another time, Garrett was shepherding a group of fugitives out of Wilmington, and again, they wanted to use the bridge across the Brandywine River at the foot of King Street. Knowing that the slave catchers had the bridge under surveillance, Garrett decided on a different strategy. He rounded up several of his bricklayer helpers. At night, the bricklayers, with two wagons, quietly slipped over the bridge. In the morning, they returned to Wilmington, but as they did so, they sang and made such a racket that they were sure to be noticed. During the day, the fugitives were hidden in the bricklayers' wagons, and when the rowdy group returned to the bridge in the evening, they kept up their song and merriment so that anyone watching would assume they were returning home after working all day. They crossed the bridge without incident.[92]

By the 1830s, there were two main tracks of the Delaware Underground Railroad. On the eastern side of the state, freedom seekers followed the route that Solomon Bayley had pioneered several decades earlier. Others followed a route from the western edge of the Great Cypress Swamp northward until both routes merged in Camden, just south of Dover. On June 4, 1830, the *Delaware Gazette and American Watchman* ran two advertisements for runaways. Jesse Eccles of Bridgeville in northern Sussex County offered $200 for the recapture of William and Jacob, who had apparently used the western route for their escape. In addition to describing the clothing they were wearing when they left Bridgeville, the advertisement typically described their physical characteristics. William, about twenty-one years old, was five feet, eight or nine inches tall, and Jacob was a little shorter. William was described as "rather black, straight and trim made, has rather a sharp voice and a down look when spoken to, no marks or scars recollected." Jacob, on the other hand, was seventeen or eighteen years old, and he was a little shorter, "his complexion rather light, has one tooth out near his eye tooth, his toe next to his largest toe is off at the first joint, occasioned by dropping a stick of wood on it."[93]

The other advertisement concerned a fugitive named Park Dennis, who left Samuel McMullen's farm south of New Castle and, like Jacob, had a variety of physical deformities: "a scar on his forehead occasioned by the kick of a horse, a finger on one of his hands off at the first joint with nail on the end of it, his left arm recently broken by a cart running over it." Tellingly, McMullen added, "He is supposed to have gone to Philadelphia or towards West Chester." If McMullen was correct in his estimation of the fugitive's goal, Dennis probably passed through Wilmington. The same could be said about William and Jacob.[94]

By the beginning of the 1830s, the Delaware network of escape routes was taking shape, and then a new form of transportation was developed that revolutionized travel and gave the Underground Railroad its name. On July 4, 1828, Charles Carroll of Carrollton, the last surviving signer of the Declaration of Independence, one of the richest men in America and the owner of several hundred enslaved people, laid the cornerstone of the Baltimore and Ohio Railroad on the west side of the city. The first cars were pulled by horses, but steam power had already demonstrated the practicality of propelling ships, and in 1830, the horses were replaced by a small steam locomotive. For the first time, land travel was not limited by the speed of an animal, and the Baltimore and Ohio Railroad proved immensely successful. The revolutionary advance in speed made railroads the epitome of fast and easy travel. The Baltimore and Ohio Railroad was soon followed by other train companies that were mostly short lines. In 1829, the Chesapeake and Delaware Canal opened across the northern Delmarva Peninsula, and to compete with the canal, the New Castle and Frenchtown Railroad began operations in 1831. Like the Baltimore and Ohio, the New Castle and Frenchtown Railroad first used horses to pull its cars but quickly switched to steam locomotives to link the two bays. The Chesapeake and Delaware Canal had several sets of locks that enabled barges and small sailing vessels to travel between the two bays, but this manmade waterway created another impediment for freedom seekers. There were a few bridges over the canal, but these were carefully watched by slave catchers.

With the growing popularity of railroads, the name became applied to the escape routes used by fugitives. It implied a quick, secret route to freedom. Sometimes, it was not quick, but the secrecy of the route remains to this day. Unlike the aboveground railroad, the Underground Railroad had no central organization, no bylaws and no official routes. Conductors and stationmasters did what they thought was right whenever they encountered a freedom seeker.[95] The Underground Railroad in Delaware, as elsewhere, developed between two convenient points that gradually become connected by a network.

WILLIAM STILL: FOR LIBERTY AND IMPROVEMENT

William Still was born on October 7, 1821, in Burlington County, New Jersey, which stretched from the Delaware River opposite Philadelphia to the Atlantic Ocean. Enslaved Africans arrived in Burlington County when it was a Dutch colony. People in bondage continued to be imported by the English when they took New Jersey from the Dutch. By 1790, the county had the largest free Black population in New Jersey, and in 1804, the state legislature passed a gradual absolution law that mirrored Pennsylvania's earlier law. All enslaved persons born after July 4, 1804, would be free. The Still family homestead was about seven miles east of Medford, a small town about a dozen miles east of Philadelphia. The area was sparsely settled by farmers who supported themselves by chopping wood, burning charcoal, digging marl and harvesting cranberries. Although William was free by New Jersey law, his mother, Charity, and two of his older sisters were enslaved when they escaped from slavery from Maryland nearly twenty years before William was born. Like many people who had once been held in bondage, the Still family guarded their family background in case an overly zealous slave hunter happened to visit the area.

As with most farm families, when William was old enough, he helped on the family farm that raised corn, rye, potatoes and other vegetables. The area was populated by a number of Quakers, who hired the Still boys during the harvest time, treated them fairly and paid good wages.[96]

Like Thomas Garrett, whose antislavery sentiments were galvanized by the kidnapping and rescue of a family household servant, William Still experienced an awakening. One of Still's neighbors, a bachelor named Thomas Wilkins, employed a fugitive who was determined not to be recaptured alive. A gang of slave hunters tracked the fugitive to the Wilkins home and broke into the house. They pounced on the fugitive and beat him with their fists until they finally were able to fasten handcuffs around one of his wrists. As they were attempting to lock the handcuffs on his other wrist, Wilkins and his two sisters arrived at the home. Someone picked up a fire shovel, ran it into the coals of the fireplace and threw the glowing embers into the middle of the slave hunters. In the panic that followed, the fugitive swung the handcuffs like a weapon and drove the slave hunters out of the house. Fearing the slave catchers would return, William Still and his brother-in-law located a hiding place for the fugitive, who had been badly cut in the brawl. Despite a heavy rainstorm, the freedom seeker and Still made their way through the pine forests of southern New Jersey until they reached the vicinity of Egg Harbor, about twenty miles away.[97]

The incident left a lasting impression on Still, who learned to read and write while on his father's farm. His abolitionist sentiments continued to grow when he subscribed to the *Colored American*, an antislavery newspaper published by Black Americans in New York. William's father died in 1842, and two years later, Still moved to Philadelphia, where he

William Still interviewed hundreds of freedom seekers at the Pennsylvania Anti-Slavery Society. *From Siebert*, Underground Railroad.

worked in sundry jobs for three years until he applied for a job as a clerk at the Pennsylvania Anti-Slavery Society. Still was required to submit a letter when applying for the job to give the hiring committee a sample of his penmanship and literacy. In his letter, Still wrote:

> *Dear Sir: I have duly considered your proposal to me, and I have come to the conclusion of availing myself of the privilege, esteeming it no small honor, to be placed in a position where I shall be considered an intelligent being, notwithstanding the salary maybe small....I have viewed the matter in various ways, but have only come to the one conclusion at last, and that is this: If I am not directly required, perhaps it may be the means of more than rewarding me in some future days. I go for liberty and improvement.*[98]

William Still got the job.

As a clerk, Still took notes of the names and physical descriptions of each freedom seeker who came into the office seeking help. One summer day in 1850, two Black men entered Still's office. One was an acquaintance of Still, and the other was Peter Friedman, a freeman who appeared to be fifty or sixty years old.[99] Freidman began to tell his story: "I am from Alabama. I have come in search of my people. I and my little brother were kidnapped about forty years ago, and I though by coming to Philadelphia and having notices written and read in the colored churches, old people would remember about it and I could find my mother and people." Still then began to question Friedman: "Where were you kidnapped from?"

"I don't know."

"Don't you know the name of the place?"

"No."

"Don't you know the name of any town, river, neighborhood or state?"

"No."

Still went on to question Friedman about his family, and he told the clerk that he had a brother, Levin, who had died from the aftereffects of a severe beating.[100] At first, Still took notes on what Friedman said, but as he told his life's story, Still stopped writing. Then the clerk told his friend that he would look into Friedman's story later and that he would find him a place to stay that night. As Still's friend began to leave, he assured the nervous Friedman that he was in good hands, but when Still continued to stare at Friedman, he became increasingly agitated. Was this clerk in league with the slave catchers?[101] A full hour passed as Still completed other clerical duties; all the while, he plied Friedman with questions. Friedman grew more perplexed.

Peter Steel, who was kidnapped as a child and remained enslaved for four decades. *From Still, Underground Rail Road.*

Finally, Still said to Friedman, "I think I can tell you about your kinfolk—mother, father." Then Still announced, "You are an own brother of mine."[102]

The dumbfounded Friedman could not believe what Still was saying. Still began to recite his family's history of how his parents, Sidney and Levin, fled from slavery, leaving behind two young boys, Peter and Levin. Still told Friedman that his parents changed their name from "Steel" to "Still," and Sidney changed her first name from Sidney to Charity, just as Peter had changed his last name from Steel to Freidman to honor two Jewish brothers who had helped him earn his freedom. He told Peter that his father had died, but his mother was alive with five of his brothers and three sisters.[103] By this happy coincidence, the living members of the Still family were reunited, and William Still dedicated his work in the antislavery office to collecting information about freedom seekers in the hope that they, too, might be reunited with their loved ones. In his interviews, he asked why fugitives ran away and the place from which they were fleeing. During the fourteen years that he did this, Still interviewed nearly one thousand fugitives. His work in the antislavery office also brought him into contact with Thomas Garrett and other prominent abolitionists. Still's Philadelphia office became the effective northern terminus of the Delaware Underground Railroad. From there, fugitives were dispersed. The freedom seekers had to decide whether they would settle in the Philadelphia area or move farther north to insulate themselves from the slave catchers. Many of the fugitives continued on their way to Canada before they felt that they were safe from recapture.

ESCAPE OF FREDERICK DOUGLASS

After the brutal lashing of Hester, young Fred Bailey witnessed many other atrocities on his owner's plantation. Bailey, however, was spared most of the physical punishments, but he was destined to experience the cruelty of slavery in other ways. The adult enslaved people received as their monthly allowance of food eight pounds of pork, or the equivalent in fish, and a

An enslaved person staked out for flogging. *From Still,* Underground Rail Road.

bushel of cornmeal. An adult's yearly clothing was designed for durability and consisted of two coarse linen shirts, one pair of linen trousers, one jacket, a pair of winter trousers made of rough "Negro" cloth, a pair of shoes and stockings. When the field work was done, enslaved laborers had to wash and mend their clothing before they went to sleep. No beds were provided for them. Men and women slept together in a common bed on the floor, covering themselves with crude blankets. In the morning, they were awakened by the sound of the driver's horn, which signaled that it was time to report to the field for the day's work. If any of the enslaved laborers were late, they faced a whipping with the dreaded cowskin.[104]

As they went about their endless tasks, the enslaved laborers often sang. According to Frederick Douglass, "I have often been astonished, since I came to the North, to find persons who could speak of singing among slaves as evidence of their contentment and happiness. It is impossible to conceive of a greater mistake. Slaves sing most when they are most unhappy. The songs of the slaves represent the sorrows of the heart; and he is relieved by them, only as an aching heart is relieved by its tears."[105]

The small children who were not old enough to do field work drove the cows back in the evening, kept the birds out of the garden, ensured the front yard was clean and ran errands for their owners and other white adults. As an adult, Bailey remembered being hungry as a child, and unlike the adult enslaved people, the children were almost naked, with only a prickly linen knee-length shirt to wear—they were given no shoes, socks, jackets or trousers to ward off the winter cold. Bailey had no bed except for the hiding place in the kitchen where he witnessed his aunt Hester's flogging. On cold nights, Bailey would pilfer a bag that was used to carry corn to the mill, crawl inside, his head and bare sticking feet out, and sleep on the cold, hard floor.[106] Bailey's home was charmless. His mother was dead, his grandmother lived a distance away and his two sisters and a brother lived in the same house, but he had little contact with them. It is little wonder that Fred had no regrets when he learned that he was going to live with the family of one of his owner's Baltimore relatives.[107] At this time, Baltimore followed Philadelphia as the nation's second-largest city; they each had a population of about eighty thousand. Each had a sizable free Black population, but unlike Philadelphia, whose enslaved population was quickly shrinking, Baltimore maintained a significant enslaved population, as Maryland was a slave state.

Bailey sailed from the Eastern Shore on one of his owner's sloops that carried a herd of sheep. He arrived on a Sunday morning at Fell's Point, one of the oldest sections of Baltimore. Sticking out like a crooked finger into the Northwest Branch of the Patapsco River, Fell's Point was home to narrow brick houses with peaked roofs and dormer windows. Many of the houses butted up against one another with a ground-level passageway that led to the back alley. After driving the boat's cargo of sheep to the slaughterhouse,

Baltimore was home to a large free Black community. *Courtesy of the Library of Congress.*

Bailey was taken to the Alice Ann (now known as Aliceanna) Street home of the family who were to be his new owners.[108] Almost at once, he noticed a marked difference in the treatment of the enslaved in the city from that of those on the farms of the Eastern Shore. An enslaved person in Baltimore was much better clothed and fed. Among the white residents of the city, there was a vestige of shame for the harsh slave owner, and it resulted in a hint of decency that checked the blatant cruelty of the plantation. Many city slave owners feared the loss of their reputation among their non–slave owning neighbors.[109]

Bailey's new owner and his wife had a young son named Thomas who was about the same age as nine-year-old Bailey. Years later, Frederick recalled, "Little Thomas was told there was his Freddy. I was told to take care of Little Thomas and thus entered upon the duties of my new home with the most cheering prospect ahead."[110] Freddy's new mistress, "a woman of the kindest heart and finest feelings," began to teach young Bailey the alphabet, and he was soon able to learn to read and spell words of three or four letters.[111] When her husband found out, however, he told her stop and said it was unlawful and unsafe to teach an enslaved person to read. He said:

> *If you give a n—r an inch, he will take an ell* [an antiquated measurement equal to forty-five inches]. *A n—r should know*

nothing but to obey his master—to do as he is told to do. Learning would spoil the best n—r in the world.*…If you teach…a n—r how to read, there would be no keeping him. It would forever unfit him to be a slave. He would at once become unmanageable, and of no value to his master. As to himself, it could do him no good, but a great deal of harm. It would make him discontented and unhappy.*[112]

Although Freddy's mistress followed her husband's instructions and stopped teaching him to read, the young enslaved boy was more determined than ever to become literate.

Bailey lived in Baltimore for seven years, and during that time, he made friends with white boys, whom Freddy turned into teachers to assist him in his quest to learn to read and write. Bailey's idyllic life—for an enslaved person—was suddenly interrupted when his legal owner on the Eastern Shore died without a will, and it became necessary to evaluate the deceased man's property to divide it among his heirs. To do this, it was necessary to bring all his enslaved laborers together. Bailey was returned to the Eastern Shore:

We were all ranked together at the valuation. Men and women, old and young, married and single, were ranked with horses, sheep, and swine. There, horses and men, cattle and women, pigs and children, all holding the same rank in the scale of being and were all subjected to the same narrow examination. Silvery-headed age and sprightly youth, maids and matrons, had to undergo the same indelicate inspection. At this moment, I saw more clearly than ever the brutalizing effects of slavery upon both slave and slaveholder.[113]

The enslaved had as much say in the matter as the horses and cattle that surrounded them. As fortune would have it, Bailey was included in the portion of the estate that was assigned to his dead owner's relatives in Baltimore, and he was returned to Fell's Point. But his stay was short-lived.

In March 1832, Freddy, now fourteen years old, was again taken back to the Eastern Shore and ordered to work as a farmhand. Freddy's relatively easy life in Baltimore did little to prepare him for the harsh life of enslavement on a farm, and it made Bailey yearn for his freedom more. In 1834, he planned his escape.

The plan was simple. Bailey and four of his compatriots would take a small boat, paddle northward on the Chesapeake Bay and eventually make

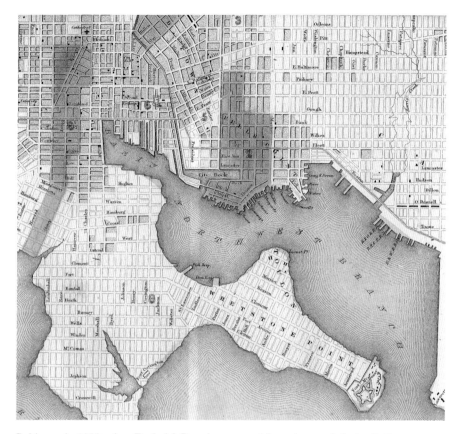

Baltimore in 1838, when Frederick Douglass escaped from slavery. *Author's collection.*

their way to Philadelphia. Fred had noticed that small steamboats headed for Philadelphia traveled northward. If they traveled by land, "anyone having a white face…could stop us, and subject us to examination."[114] The one advantage that Bailey had was that he was literate, a fact that he usually kept to himself. A week before the planned escape, Bailey wrote out passes for each of the freedom seekers that said: "This is to certify that I, the undersigned, have given the bearer my servant full liberty to go to Baltimore and spend the Easter Holidays."[115] As Bailey thought about running away, "the frightful liability of being returned to slavey—with the certainty of being treated tenfold worse than before—the thought was a truly horrible one, and one which it was not easy to overcome."[116] Bailey and his companions had all experienced firsthand all the horrors of slavery, and Frederick mused, "On the other hand, away back in the dim

The sale of enslaved people tore families apart. *Courtesy of the Library of Congress.*

distance, under the flickering light of the North Star, behind some craggy hill or snow-covered mountain, stood a doubtful freedom—half frozen—beckoning us to come share its hospitality."[117]

Bailey spent the last couple of days before his planned escape fretting over every facet of the plan, examining every detail and assuaging the fears of his comrades. After several days of fitful waiting, the agreed-upon Saturday morning arrived, and Frederick and the other freedom seekers followed their normal routine. The horn was blown for breakfast, and the enslaved went to the house to eat. As Bailey approached the house, he spotted two men on horseback leading two Black men with their hands tied. When they reached the gate, the two white men got off their horses and tied the two Black men to the gate post. At this point, several white men on horseback appeared and rode to the barn and back. Bailey had gone into the kitchen of the house when three constables rode up. Frederick was told that some men wanted to see him, and when he went to the door, the constables grabbed him and tied his hands closely together. The constables told Frederick that there had been a "scrape" and that his owner wanted to question him. They told Bailey that if he told the truth, he would not be hurt.[118]

One by one, Bailey's fellow freedom seekers were apprehended. In the confusion, Bailey managed to pass the word to "own nothing" (to admit to nothing) to his fellow freedom seekers. The conspirators managed to destroy their incriminating passes without being observed. Bailey pitched his into the fireplace. One of the others ate his with a biscuit. After the would-be fugitives were rounded up, they were taken to Easton, where they were placed in the jail behind the brick courthouse. A swarm of grinning slave traders descended on the jail, making rude comments and taunting the captured freedom seekers as they tried to assess their value. The supposed ringleader, Bailey, was left in the jail while the others were taken home. Bailey was told that a slave trader from Alabama was on his way to purchase the failed runaway and take him to a plantation in the Deep South. For several days, Frederick sat in the jail cell, contemplating his exile to a plantation where there would be no hope of escape. The slave trader from Alabama, however, never appeared. To Bailey's astonishment, he was to be sent to Baltimore to live with the family who had used him to look after their young son, Thomas. Like Bailey, Thomas was now a teenager, and he had no need for Freddy to watch over him. The father of the family wanted no work from Bailey, and he hired Frederick out to Gardiner's shipyard on Fell's Point.[119]

At that time, two brigs were being built at the shipyard, and Gardiner ordered Bailey to do whatever the carpenters ordered him to do. In effect, he became a carpenter's apprentice, and he had seventy-five men acting as his master. According to Bailey, "It was, 'Fred, help; can't [move] this timber here….Fred, come help saw off the end of this timber….Fred, go quick and get the crowbar….Halloo, n—r! Come turn this grindstone…. Come, come, move, move….Hold on where you are! Damn you, if you move, I'll blow your brains out.'"[120]

Bailey was in Gardiner's shipyard for about eight months when he got into a brawl with four white apprentices. Many of the carpenters were free Black men, and their numbers appeared to be growing. The white carpenters feared that they would crowd them out of their jobs. The white apprentices also felt that working with Black men was degrading. According to Bailey, "They began to put on airs, and talk about the 'n—rs' taking the country, saying we all ought to be killed."[121] Several times, one of the white apprentices attacked Bailey, but he fought back and was able to defend himself. Eventually, the white apprentices attacked Bailey with sticks, stones, handspikes and a brick. "One of their number gave me, with his heavy boot, a powerful kick in the left eye. My eyeball seemed to burst. When they saw my eye closed and badly swollen, they left me." During the fight, the white carpenters watched and called out, "Kill the damned n——r! Kill him! Kill him! He struck a white person!"[122]

Fortunately, Bailey was able to escape from Gardiner's shipyard without further injury. After he recovered from his wounds, Frederick went to work in another shipyard as a caulker, a workman who hammered oakum or other fibrous material into the seams between a ship's planks to make them watertight. This was done on the hull and deck planks. The process was relatively simple, but it took a degree of finesse. The oakum was prepared by being rolled into a long strand. The caulker then used a caulking iron, shaped somewhat like a chisel but with a wider and blunter blade, to shove one end of the strand into the seam. He then took a wooden mallet to tap the rest of strand of oakum into the seam by dropping down a few inches on the strand and sliding it up and tapping it into the seam. With a few feet of the loosely packed oakum in the seam, the calker would drive the oakum home with a sharp hit of the mallet, being careful not to drive it too hard, which could cause the oakum to push out of the inside of the seam. While the caulkers were at work, there was a steady *tap-tap-tap* echoing about the vessel. The caulkers usually kept two mallets with them. One was placed in a bucket of water or tied to a light line and thrown into the water beside the vessel. On hot days, when the mallet dried out, the ring at the end of the mallet that kept the wood from splitting would become loose. If it slid too far to the end of the mallet, the striking metal on metal could send dangerous metal splinters flying that would cause dangerous sores if they became embedded in the caulker's hands or eyes. When the caulker felt that the ring was getting loose, they would switch to the other mallet that was sitting in the water, which made the wood swell and the rings tight. Years later, Bailey recalled, "Very soon, [I] learned the art of using my mallet and irons."[123]

Black workers dominated the caulking trade on Fell's Point, and in 1838, they formed the Caulkers Association, one America's first Black trade unions. The Black caulkers also formed the East Baltimore Mental Improvement Society to teach people how to read and write. Bailey joined the group, and he took an active part in the society's debates. Bailey found his short experience with the society intellectually liberating, and he later wrote, "I owe much to the society of these young men."[124] Caulking was a vital part of building a wooden ship, but at times, it could be monotonous work. This gave Bailey time to think while he was hammering the oakum home with his

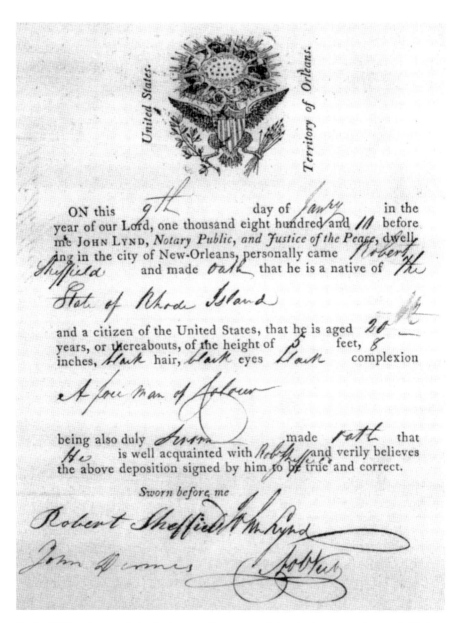

Frederick Douglass carried sailor's protection papers. A handwritten note that reads, "A free man of color," can be seen in the center. *Courtesy of the Library of Congress.*

mallet. He had plenty to consider: the debates at the society, his status as an enslaved person and his plans for his next escape attempt.

In Maryland and other slave states, free persons of color were required to carry papers that indicated they were not enslaved. Any white person, at any time and for any reason—or for no reason—could stop a Black person and demand to see their papers. If the person of color could not produce their papers, then the presumption was that they were a fugitive and could be arrested. These "free papers" listed the person's name, age, skin color, height and general appearance. Such free papers were in high demand for enslaved people contemplating an escape, and often times, free Black Americans would give escapees their papers to use in their flights for freedom. Once the fugitives were free, these papers would be returned to their original owner. This arrangement was dangerous for both parties. The failure to return the papers to their original owners could be disastrous for them. Without the papers, they were in danger of being sold into slavery. The freedom seeker ran the risk of capture if the description on the papers did not match their appearance. As Frederick Douglass remarked, "It was, therefore, an act of supreme trust on the part of a freeman of color this to put in jeopardy his own liberty that another might be free." Douglass also remarked, "It was not, however, unfrequently, bravely done and was seldom discovered."[125]

Bailey had a friend who had "sailor's protection papers" that were used to verify their nationality while they were at sea as a protection against being impressed aboard a foreign vessel. Adorned with a large American eagle, this certificate contained a physical description of its owner, and in this case, it described a man who was much darker than Bailey. The certificate also indicated that this man was free. Bailey's friend agreed to let him borrow his sailor's protection certificate to document that he was a free person of color. With this certificate in hand, Bailey began to hatch a plan for his second attempt at gaining his freedom. He had his fiancée, Anna Murray, make a set of sailor's clothing, including a red shirt, tarpaulin hat (a common sailor's hat that was made of straw or canvas and covered with a thin coating of pitch or black paint) and a black scarf tied loosely around his neck, so that he would be "rigged in sailor style." Bailey felt that Baltimore's association with sailors and the recent War of 1812 that was fought partially over "free trade and sailors' rights" might engender him some sympathy. Fort McHenry, the inspiration for Francis Scott Keys's "Star-Spangled Banner," was a short distance across the northwest branch of the Patapsco River and could be seen from Fell's Point. Although Bailey had not been to sea, he believed that during his work as a caulker, he learned "a ship from stem to stern, from keelson to cross-trees, and could talk sailor like an 'old salt.'"[126]

In addition to taking the help of Anna, Baily enlisted a trusted friend for a carefully choreographed escape plan that involved the aboveground railroad and a dangerous segment of the Delaware Underground Railroad. Train service had greatly expanded since the first tracks of the Baltimore and Ohio Railroad were laid to Ellicott City. While the Baltimore and Ohio Railroad was steadily making its way westward, the Philadelphia, Wilmington and Baltimore Railroad was being constructed to connect the Pennsylvania city with Baltimore. In 1838, there were still important gaps in the tracks, particularly across the Susquehanna River and from Wilmington to Philadelphia. These two breaks in the tracks would present Bailey with particular dangers of recapture.

On Monday morning, September 3, 1838, Frederick and Anna went to the train depot on the edge of Baltimore to begin what award-wining historian David. W. Bright called "the most famous escape in the annals of American slavery."[127] In order to avoid careful scrutiny at the train depot, Bailey arranged for his baggage to held by a friend around the corner from the train depot. Bailey feared that if he bought a ticket ahead of time, he would be subjected to intense scrutiny, and his escape would be quashed before it started. Instead, he remained in the background as the other passengers boarded the train cars. Once they were all aboard and the train began to move, he quickly approached the train, and as the cars began to gain speed, he hopped on board. At the same time, his friend appeared and handed his luggage to him as the small engine pulled the cars forward.

On the train and armed with the borrowed sailor's pass and a concocted story to explain why he did not have any free papers, Bailey calmly took a seat in the car assigned to people of color and waited until the conductor arrived so he could purchase a ticket. The train was well on its way toward the northern end of the Chesapeake Bay when the conductor arrived in Bailey's car to collect tickets and examine the papers of the Black passengers. Bailey noticed that the conductor was abrupt and harsh when he spoke to the other Black riders, and he was apprehensive as the conductor approached him. The freedom seeker's future depended on the decision of the conductor. A hint of suspicion would lead to Bailey's arrest, and this time, he would not be so lucky to be released to a friendly owner in Baltimore. Instead, he would be sentenced to a lifetime of hard labor. As the conductor came closer, Bailey noticed a change in his demeanor. Perhaps it was the fugitive's sailor's attire. Perhaps it was Bailey's relaxed manner that contrasted with the others who

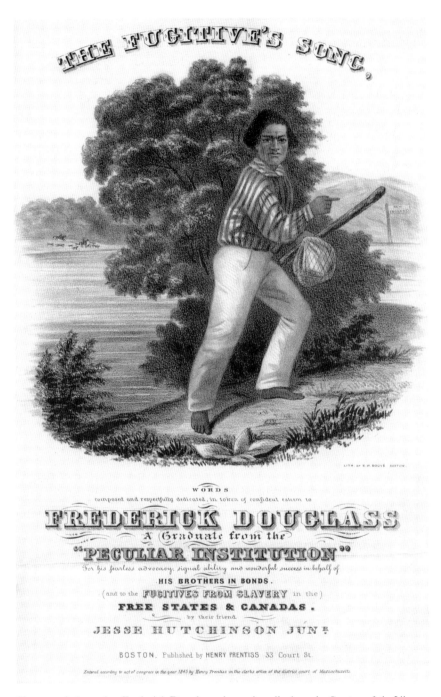

Sheet music honoring Frederick Douglass, shown in sailor's garb. *Courtesy of the Library of Congress.*

had readily produced their papers on the conductor's approach. Looking at Bailey, the conductor asked, "I suppose you have your free papers?"

Knowing that he did not and would most likely be asked this on his trip north, Bailey answered with the well-thought-out story he had prepared: "No, sir, I never carry my free papers to sea with me." The conductor then asked, "But you have something to show that you are a free man, have you not?"

"Yes, I have a paper with the American eagle on it that will carry me around the world." With that, Bailey reached into his pocket and withdrew his borrowed sailor's protection certificate. The conductor glanced at the paper and at Bailey, and he failed to notice that the description on the certificate did not match the freedom seeker. Bailey paid his fare, and the conductor went about his business.[128]

Bailey spotted several other passengers on the train whom he thought he knew, but they failed to recognize him dressed as a sailor. Running parallel to the western shore of the Chesapeake Bay, where most of the rivers are wide but relatively shallow, the railroad company had been able to build bridges over them. Bailey watched as he crossed the Back and Gunpowder Rivers until he reached the town of Havre de Grace and the Susquehanna River, which had not yet been bridged. On the south side of the river, all the passengers disembarked from the train and boarded a ferryboat to carry them across the river. On the other side, a train waited for them that would take them to Wilmington, Delaware. On board the ferry, Bailey ran into a curious Black deckhand who kept asking him questions about where he was going, when was he coming back, et cetera. And these questions came dangerously close to exposing Bailey as a fugitive. Having been questioned more thoroughly by the deckhand than he had by any of the white people he had encountered, the freedom seeker went to another part of the boat to avoid any further interrogation.[129]

Once he left the ferryboat and boarded the northbound train, Bailey looked over to a southbound train that had just arrived to unload the passengers for the ferry across the Susquehanna. There, he spotted the owner of a boat he had worked on a few days before. Had the owner gotten a good look at Bailey, he would have recognized him, but in the bustle of changing to the ferryboat, he did not. Once on the train, Bailey encountered yet another man, a German blacksmith, whom the fugitive knew well. He looked directly at Bailey, who thought he saw a glimmer of recognition in the blacksmith's face. The fugitive caulker believed that the blacksmith had recognized him, but he apparently decided not to betray him. Years later, Fred recalled, "Minutes were hours, and hours were days during this part

Left: The railroad
line from Baltimore
to Philadelphia.
*Courtesy of the
Delaware Public
Archives.*

Opposite: Young
Frederick Douglass.
*Courtesy of the Library
of Congress.*

of my flight, After Maryland, I was to pass through Delaware—another slave state, where slave catchers generally awaited their prey, for it was not in the interior of the state but on its borders that these human hounds were most vigilant and active. The border lines between slavery and freedom were the most dangerous ones for the fugitives."[130]

Finally, the train crossed into Delaware, and in a matter of minutes, it pulled into Wilmington, where Bailey had additional hurdles to overcome. It was "the last point of imminent danger and the one I dread most."[131] Apparently, Bailey did not know of Thomas Garrett and his network of assistants who were ready to spirit any fugitive to safety. Bailey was not about to approach any stranger, Black or white, unless he had to. The train stopped in the middle of town, not far from the steamboat landing, and the passengers walked as a group to meet the boat for Philadelphia. No one questioned the young Black man dressed as sailor, who had taken advantage of the aboveground railroad for a momentary trip on Delaware's Underground Railroad. After boarding the steamboat, Frederick was "on the broad and beautiful Delaware speeding away to the Quaker city."[132] That night, in Philadelphia, Bailey boarded the train for New York, and he arrived in the morning, having completed his nearly two-hundred-mile-long journey to freedom in less than twenty-four hours. Anna joined Frederick in New York, where they were married. From there, the newlyweds moved on to the port of New Bedford, where Bailey hoped to find work as a caulker.

As was the custom with many escaped enslaved people, Bailey chose a new name to hide his identity and make it difficult to track him. When he was born, his mother had named him Frederick Augustus Washington Bailey; while in Baltimore, he dropped "Washington Augustus" and was known simply as Frederick Bailey. He decided to keep Frederick as his first name and initially chose Johnson as his last name. As it happened, Frederick was staying with a man named Nathan Johnson, and Frederick believed that in "New Bedford, the Johnson family was already so numerous as to cause some confusion in distinguishing one from another; change to this name seemed desirable."[133] Nathan Johnson, Frederick's host, had just finished the epic poem *Lady of the Lake* by Sir Walter Scott. He was impressed by the character of James Douglas and suggested that Frederick adopt Douglas as his last name. After reading the poem, Frederick agreed, but he added an "s" to the name, and Frederick Augustus Washington Bailey, one of the most distinguished passengers on the Delaware Underground Railroad, became Frederick Douglass.[134]

Escape of the Hawkins Family

Had Frederick Douglass waited a few months, he could have avoided his brief foray on the Delaware Underground Railroad through Wilmington that he feared so much. In December 1838, the Philadelphia, Wilmington and Baltimore Railroad completed the construction of its tracks from Wilmington into Philadelphia and eliminated the need for train passengers to disembark at Wilmington and take a steamboat to the City of Brotherly Love. Freedom seekers continued to take the train through Delaware, but their passage was so brief that they are usually not counted as having ridden on the Underground Railroad. In addition, railroad officials were aware that fugitives were using their cars to escape to Pennsylvania, and they began to tighten security measures around Black passengers. The flow of freedom seekers on foot through Delaware and Wilmington continued, however, and Thomas Garrett continued to help them. He assisted more and more fugitives, and by 1845, he had helped over one thousand on their way to freedom.[135]

Samuel Hawkins's wife, Emeline (called "Em"), was enslaved, as were their six children: Chester, eighteen; Samuel, fourteen; Sally Ann, about seven or eight; Washington, whose age is unknown; a boy whose age and name are unknown; and a toddler who was about eighteen months old who lived in Queen Anne's County, Maryland, which bordered Delaware north of Talbot and Caroline Counties, Maryland. Samuel was a free man, but Em and her six children were all enslaved by various owners. Samuel tried to buy Em's freedom, but her owner refused. Two days after Christmas 1845, Samuel, Em and their six children decided to flee to Delaware. They secured a covered wagon that was drawn by Sam's horse and the help of Samuel D. Burris, who lived in the vicinity of Camden, Delaware, south of Dover. Burris was born to free parents in 1813, near Willow Grove in Kent County, Delaware, about ten miles southwest of Camden. Burris was familiar with the stations between Dover and the Maryland border. Em and the four younger children rode in the wagon while Sam and the teenage boys

Samuel Burris aided the Hawkins family. *From Still,* Underground Rail Road.

walked. Along the way, they were joined by four other freedom seekers, making the party one of thirteen. The Hawkins family headed due east into Delaware and Camden, where Burris received a letter of introduction from Ezekiel Jenkins, a Quaker, to John Hunn and others who lived in Middletown, Delaware. On the second night of their trip, the group of freedom seekers encountered a severe snowstorm, but in the morning, the weather cleared and the sun glistened off the deep snow as the nearly frozen fugitives made their way past Thomas Merritt's house and toward John Hunn's farm. Hunn had never before assisted fugitives, but it was decided that the fugitive party would stay at his farm until the roads were in better shape to travel. Not only were the fugitives weary, but one of the men was also suffering from frostbite, and his foot was frozen to his boot. Only after the boot was soaked in water was he able to get it off. Hunn had breakfast prepared, and after they had eaten, Em and the four younger children remained in the house, and the men went to the barn to sleep in the hay.

In the afternoon, Thomas Merritt showed up at Hunn's house and asked if Hunn had seen any strange Black people lurking about. Merritt had either spotted the Haskins party or had seen the tracks of the wagon and their footprints in the snow. In the late afternoon, four white men, one of whom was Richard C. Hayes, a constable from Middletown, north of Dover, arrived in a sleigh. The men asked Hunn if he had seen any strange Black people. Hunn said he had, and one of the white men said that they were runaways. Hunn asked how he knew that. The man pulled out an advertisement for some runaways that offered a $1,000 reward for three fugitives who may have been three of the four men who had joined the Haskins party on their way into Delaware—or it may have been about some unrelated fugitives. In any case, the men began to nose around the farm buildings when they spotted Sam Hawkins, who ran toward the house. Hunn and the others gave chase, and they cornered Hawkins near the house. When Hawkins brandished a large knife, the constable answered by pulling out a pistol and threatening to shoot Hawkins. The constable, Hays, told Hunn to get the knife, but the Quaker refused to take an active role in capturing the freedom seekers. Hawkins agreed to surrender the knife if the constable would give Hunn his pistol. When the confrontation quieted, Hawkins produced his papers, but the slave catchers pronounced them a forgery, and the rest of the party was rounded up and taken to a magistrate in Middletown.

At the magistrate's office, the slave catchers proposed to let Samuel, his wife and four younger children go if he would allow them to take the teenage boys back to Maryland, but it was only a ruse to get Em and the children into the jail. Meanwhile, the judge declared the paperwork was not defective and released everyone. And they again began their trek to Wilmington and eventual freedom.[136]

John Hunn aided the Hawkins family. *From Still*, Underground Rail Road.

THE TRIAL OF SAMUEL BURRIS, JOHN HUNN AND THOMAS GARRETT

After the Hawkins group successfully escaped, the troubles for Samuel Burris, John Hunn and Thomas Garrett were not over. All three men became known as agents on the Delaware Underground Railroad, and the state's slave owners and their sympathizers were out to get them. In 1847, two years after the Hawkins incident, Burris was charged with aiding other fugitives. Tried at New Castle, he was found guilty and sentenced to be sold into slavery. The abolitionists of Pennsylvania raised money to purchase Burris when the auction was held on November 2, 1847. John Hunn and Thomas Garrett were too well known, so Isaac S. Flint, a trusted Wilmington abolitionist, was recruited to pose as a slave trader so he could buy Burris at the sale. Cool, fearless and well-versed in the behavior of slave traders at auctions, Flint was the perfect choice to buy Burris. At the auction in front of the Dover Courthouse, Burris was led to the auction block. Included in the crowd of potential buyers were a number of slave traders and Flint. The traders examined Burris from head to toe, as if they were jockeys examining a potential mount. In the parade of slave traders that examined Burris was Flint, who went through the motions expertly, as if he were a veteran of such sales. After the bidding started, Flint had to be careful that he entered the bidding at the right time so as not to drive the price beyond the amount the abolitionists had collected. It was whispered to Burris to not be afraid,

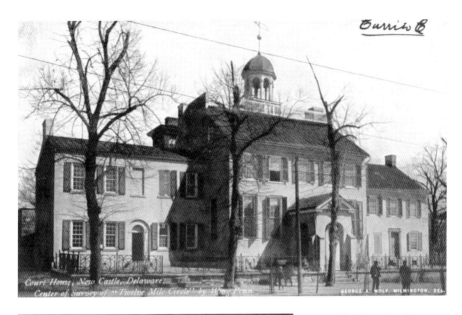

Above: The New Castle Courthouse, where the trial of Thomas Garrett, John Hunn and Samuel Burris was held. *Courtesy of the Delaware Public Archives.*

Left: Supreme Court chief justice Roger B. Taney presided over the trials of those involved in the Hawkins family's escape. *Courtesy of the Library of Congress.*

that he was being bought by a friend. Finally, the sale was closed, with Flint having the winning bid of $500.

Burris was immediately hustled off to Philadelphia, where he rejoined his family. Not feeling safe and having an opportunity to join the gold rush, Burris moved to California. And when California entered the Union as a free state, Samuel Burris was one thousand miles from the nearest slave state.[137]

Meanwhile, the former owners of the Hawkins family and the others sued Thomas Garrett and John Hunn for the loss of their property under the terms of the Fugitive Slave Law of 1793. Their trial was held in the U.S. Circuit Court of Delaware in New Castle with Chief Justice Roger B. Taney of the U.S. Supreme Court presiding. Taney was from Maryland and was a former slave owner, but his attitude toward slavery was somewhat clouded. Garrett and Hunn were charged with assisting Em Hawkins and her six children to freedom. At the conclusion of Garrett's trial, the abolitionist newspaper *Pennsylvania Freeman* reported that Chief Justice Taney charged the jury "that if it were proved that he [Garrett] had afforded the alleged slaves facilities for escape, he was guilty [italic in the original] '*although they had been set at liberty by the Court, and even if he had no reason to believe them slaves.*' With such a court—and probably with a thoroughly proslavery jury—these worthy men could not fail to be convicted, with or without proof."[138]

The *Pennsylvania Freeman* went on to report, "The jury gave a verdict against him [Garrett] and fined him $3,500. John Hunn was also fined $2,500. The claimant of the alleged fugitives then came upon Friend Garrett for *trespass* and obtained a verdict of $1,900 damages, though their own witnesses valued the slaves at only $1,600, making the full amount of the judicial robbery upon him $5,400 or $7,900 for both."[139]

The *Pennsylvania Freeman* editorialized, "We can scarcely conceive of the monstrous inhumanity and moral deformity which would refuse to aid the flying slave to escape his bondage, to feed him, to bind up his wounds, and give him rest in his weariness and speed him on his way to a land of freedom.… The judge and jury who, on any consideration, would aid in punishing as a crime such a deed as that of Thomas Garrett's should be covered with infamy, as the enemy of this kind and the ally of kidnappers."[140]

After the verdict was rendered, there was some negotiation with the plaintiffs, and the amount paid to them was considerably reduced. As people were leaving the courtroom, Garrett made a speech in which he declared, "I should have done violence to my convictions of duty had I not made use of all lawful means in my power to liberate those people and assist them to become men and women, rather than leave them in the condition of chattels personal. I am called an abolitionist, once a name of reproach, but one I have ever been proud to be considered worth of being called."[141]

The Wilmington businessman went on to say, "I have assisted over one hundred [freedom seekers] in twenty-five years on their way to the North, and I now consider the penalty imposed might be as a license for the remained of my life; but be that as it may, if any of thee know of any slave who needs assistance, send him to me, as I now publicly pledge myself to double my diligence and never neglect an opportunity to assist a slave to obtain freedom."[142]

HARRIET TUBMAN IN DELAWARE

Mr. Garrett, I am here again, out of money and with no shoes to my feet, and God has sent me to you for what I need.
—Harriet Tubman[143]

THE GREAT ESCAPE ON THE *PEARL*

By the time of Thomas Garrett's trial in 1848, the Underground Railroad had matured. In Wilmington, Garrett's cadre of helpers enabled him to identify and help many of the freedom seekers moving through the city, and he was able to give them advice, supplies and money for the last leg of their journey into Pennsylvania. Many of the fugitives were sent directly to Philadelphia, where William Still's Pennsylvania Anti-Slavery Society shuttled them to communities where they could find work and be safe. Garrett also sent fugitives directly north into Chester County, Pennsylvania, where there was another active antislavery community.

At the same time, the abolitionist movement in the North was also maturing. Unlike the Underground Railroad, which, by necessity, operated in secret, the abolitionists could freely announce their intentions to end slavery. There were several abolitionist newspapers, most notably William Lloyd Garrison's *Liberator*, the short-lived *African Observer* and Frederick Douglass's *North Star*. By the 1840s, the abolitionist movement had begun to divide into two factions. Both groups strongly advocated for the end of slavery, but one

Slave coffles were common in Washington, D.C. *Courtesy of the Library of Congress.*

faction took no direct action to make that happen, and they confined their efforts to legal routes. The other faction actively worked to liberate enslaved people without waiting for the legal system to end the practice of owning human beings. Some of the well-to-do abolitionists in the latter group used their money to assist fugitives on their journeys to freedom.

Many abolitionists were particularly disturbed by the existence of slavery in Washington, D.C. As the nation's capital, Washington was symbolic of the entire nation's values. The city had a growing free Black population, but enslaved people were held by ordinary citizens and members of all three branches of the government. Coffles of enslaved people were marched openly through the streets. Slave pens were intermixed with government buildings, and slave auctions, where men, women and children were sold like horses and cows to the highest bidders, were held a short distance from the hallowed halls of Congress. Many of the auctions' bidders were from the Deep South, where the growing cotton culture demanded more labor for their plantations. Washington was a gateway for the movement of enslaved people from Delaware, Maryland and Virginia to the Deep South, where they faced a lifelong sentence of hard labor on the expanding cotton plantations.

Freeing all the enslaved people in Washington and stopping the slave trade became a major goal of the active abolitionists, who looked for a way to focus their attention on the situation in Washington. A plan evolved for a mass escape of fifty to seventy-five enslaved people that would spotlight the incongruity of the existence of chattel labor in the capital of the "land of the free." The identities of those who financed the venture have been subjects of debate, but they probably included William Chapman, an abolitionist newspaperman, and Geritt Smith, a wealthy New Yorker who was known to have contributed to abolitionist projects.[144]

Daniel Drayton, a forty-six-year-old New Jersey native and veteran waterman on both the Delaware and Chesapeake Bays, did not move in these wealthy abolitionist circles. Instead, he spent the best years of his life traveling up and down the Atlantic coast.[145] Drayton prospered for a time, and he was able to buy a half interest in a sloop. On a trip from Baltimore to Philadelphia by way of the Delaware and Chesapeake Canal, his sloop struck a submerged tree trunk near the mouth of the Susquehanna River, and it sank within five minutes. Drayton and his crew were able to scramble onto a deck boat, and they were saved, but Drayton lost everything except for the clothes on his back.[146] Drayton's misfortunes continued when he lost another vessel off the coast of North Carolina and yet another off the coast of Long Island.[147]

During Drayton's travels, the hard luck skipper often came into contact with the enslaved population along the shores of the Chesapeake and Delaware Bays. The bay captain observed:

I know it is sometimes said by those who defend slavery or apologize for it that the slaves at the South are very happy and contented, if left to themselves, and that this idea of running away is only put into their heads by mischievous white people from the North….But there is not a waterman who ever sailed in Chesapeake Bay who will not tell you that….The difficulty is, when they ask you to assist them, to make them take no for an answer. I have known instances where men have lain in the woods for a year or two, waiting for an opportunity to escape on board some vessel.[148]

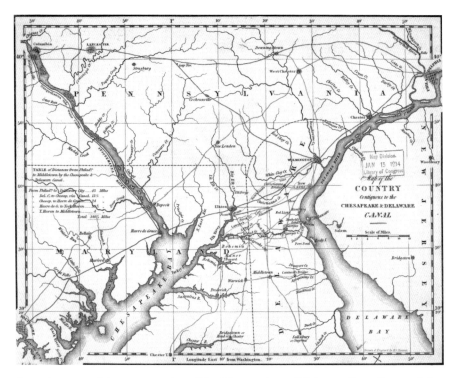

A canal connected the upper reaches of the Chesapeake and Delaware Bays. *Courtesy of the Library of Congress.*

In 1847, Drayton went to Washington to deliver a cargo of oysters. While at the dock, a Black man named Stevenson came on board, and he remarked that Drayton seemed to be from the North.[149] After a bit of further small talk about abolitionists, Stevenson told Drayton that he wanted to arrange passage to the North for a woman and five children. According to Stevenson, the husband of the woman and father of the children was a free man. Stevenson convinced the waterman take her and her five children to the North. Shortly thereafter, the woman, her five children and a niece boarded Drayton's boat, and he set sail for Frenchtown, Maryland, near the head of the Chesapeake Bay. Frenchtown was four miles north of the Chesapeake and Delaware Canal and a scant two miles west of the Delaware border.[150]

It took Drayton and his passengers ten long days to reach Frenchtown, where they met the woman's husband, who, it turns out, was Stevenson. Fortunately, Frenchtown, which was the western terminus of the transpeninsular railroad that started in New Castle, was a dying town. The canal had taken most of the commercial traffic away from the railroad, and there was not enough passenger traffic to support the train line. With its scarcity of activity, excellent boat landing and short distance from Delaware and that state's Underground Railroad, Frenchtown was a relatively secure place for freedom seekers.[151] From the Maryland town, it was only about a dozen miles across the peninsula to the Delaware River, and it had easy connections to Wilmington and Garrett's network of agents. From there, it was a relatively safe journey to Philadelphia and freedom.

After stopping at Frenchtown, Drayton eventually delivered the Stevenson family to Philadelphia.[152] This, however, was not the last Drayton heard from the abolitionists. The Stevenson family praised the waterman's efforts in transporting them from Washington, D.C., to freedom. A short time later, an abolitionist whose identity is still up for debate hired Drayton to transport a group of enslaved people from Washington, through the Chesapeake and Delaware Canal and on to Philadelphia. At this time, Drayton did not have a vessel at his disposal, but he contacted Captain Edward Sayres, who commanded a small bay schooner named the *Pearl*. Drayton proposed to charter the *Pearl* for one hundred dollars to go to Washington, pick up the fugitives and sail back to Frenchtown, where they would meet friends who would lead them along the Delaware Underground Railroad to Philadelphia. One hundred dollars was considerably more than a vessel could earn on any ordinary trip of this duration, so Sayres agreed to the plan. In Washington, Drayton was to control the passengers he allowed on board, and control of the vessel remained with Sayres. According to Drayton, "I, too, was to be paid for my time and trouble—an offer which the low state of my pecuniary affairs and the necessity of supporting my family did not allow me to decline."

The two men also agreed that Drayton would not tell Sayres the names of any of the people who were financing the expedition and that he would not have any direct communication with them in either Philadelphia or Washington. Sayres employed on the *Pearl* a young man named Chester English, who worked as cook and sailor. According to Drayton, English was "inexperienced as a child." He said, "He went with us but was kept in total ignorance of the real object of the voyage. He had the idea that we were going to Washington for a load of ship timber."[153]

The *Pearl* was a two-masted bay schooner that was about sixty-five to eighty feet long and around twenty feet wide; it could accommodate about seventy-five tightly packed fugitives. Drayton, Sayers and English were the only crewmen on board the *Pearl*.

In early April 1848, the *Pearl* left Philadelphia, traveled through the Chesapeake and Delaware Canal and down the Chesapeake Bay and entered the Potomac River. After stopping at Machudock, Virginia, to pick up a load of wood to act as a pretense for the voyage, the *Pearl* docked in Washington on Thursday, April 13. The lumber was unloaded, and provisions were taken on board. Drayton had purchased three bushels of meal, 206 pounds of pork and 15 gallons of molasses, which he calculated would be sufficient for the estimated four-day trip.[154] The great escape on the *Pearl*, one of the largest—if not the largest—mass exoduses in the history of the Underground Railroad, would shine a national spotlight on slavery in the nation's capital and ignite a hoped-for antislavery wave.

Although not universally observed, particularly for house servants, enslaved people traditionally had Sunday off, and Saturday night was chosen for the departure time in the hopes that the *Pearl* was well down the Potomac River before morning, when the freedom seekers would be missed. According to Drayton, "Shortly after dark, the expected passengers began to arrive, coming stealthily across the fields and gliding silently on board the vessel."[155] Among the freedom seekers were six siblings of the Edmondson family, four men (Ephraim, Richard, John and Samuel) and two teenage girls (Mary, fifteen years old, and Emily, thirteen years old).[156] As each of the fugitives arrived, English lifted the hatch, and after they descended into the hold, he shut it. Among the parade of freedom seekers who boarded the *Pearl* were one of former first lady Dolley Madison's servants; a coachman for Robert John Walker, the secretary of the treasury under President James Polk; and other servants from prominent Washington families. This was no ragtag band of fugitives. As Frederick Douglass pointed out, enslaved people in the city were better fed and better dressed than enslaved people on plantations. The word of the attempted escape had spread far, and before English closed the hatch for the last time, about seventy-five fugitives (the exact number is a subject of debate) were crammed into the hold of the *Pearl*.

As each of the freedom seekers climbed down the short ladder into the bowels of the schooner, they smiled and nodded as they saw familiar faces in the dimly lit hold. Many were friends, some were relatives and others were strangers. Around ten o'clock, the curfew bell rang, signaling that all Black people, slave and free, were to be off the streets of Washington.[157] Then the hatch was closed for the last time. The fugitives made themselves as comfortable as possible in the dark, cramped hold of the workboat and waited. After about two hours, the freedom seekers could hear Drayton ordering English to cast off the lines and get ready to sail. The fugitives

Small sailing craft were used by fugitives to escape to freedom. *Courtesy of the Delaware Public Archives.*

listened to the squeaky sounds of the lines passing through the pulley blocks and the clanking of the rings that attached the sails to the mast as English raised the canvas. The fugitives were underway at last. Ahead of them was a long voyage up the Chesapeake Bay to Frenchtown, where they would meet agents of the Underground Railroad who would conduct them through Delaware to the free state of Pennsylvania. On the *Pearl*, however, the freedom seekers felt no forward movement. There was no wind, and the schooner sat stationary, bobbing on the quiet Potomac. They could not feel it, but the tide was coming in. Suddenly, there was the splash of an anchor. Drayton had decided to wait for better sailing conditions.[158] Below deck, the freedom seekers had no choice but to wait and to worry. As the hours passed, the *Pearl* remained in a dead calm until the sun began to rise.[159]

The first glimmer of light shown through the loose-fitting hatches, and as the fugitives watched the dawn grow brighter, all hope of them making a fast exit from Washington was gone. Then a light north wind began to blow, and the fugitives could hear the anchor being raised and the sails flapping lightly in the breeze. Then the canvas grew taught. The rolling, bobbing motion disappeared, and the freedom seekers braced themselves as the *Pearl* began to tilt to one side. As the sun came up, the *Pearl* began to slice through the Potomac. Suddenly, the hatch was opened, and Drayton appeared. The hard luck captain went down into the hold and saw that his passengers were "thickly stowed."[160] Drayton distributed some bread to the freedom seekers and knocked down the bulkhead between the hold and the cabin to allow them to get into the cabin to cook. The *Pearl* was on its way to Delaware and freedom.

The wind increased steadily, and the *Pearl* began to zip along as the schooner ran before the wind. As the *Pearl* made its way southward on the Potomac, some of the freedom seekers sang hymns, and others read from the Bible. Mary and Emily took part in the singing, but the two Edmondson girls were illiterate and could not read the Bible passages.[161] When the sun went down on Sunday evening, the hatch covers were opened, and the freedom seekers came on deck to stretch and get some fresh air. Mary Edmondson, along with a number of the passengers, was seasick. Her brother Samuel carried her up the ladder to the deck where she could sit and lean against the foremast. He retrieved some of the provisions that the Edmondsons carried with them, including brandy, meat, rolls and tea.[162]

As the schooner neared the mouth of the Potomac, the north wind increased and drove the fugitives back into the cramped quarters of the hold. The north wind continued to strengthen to the point that it was impossible to make a turn into the wind to head up the Chesapeake Bay. There were only a few choices: anchor in a quiet place in the Potomac and wait for the wind to change or continue out into the bay and turn southward toward the Atlantic. Drayton did not want to stay put. He knew that they had taken too long to reach the bay. The owners of many of the enslaved had probably reported them missing, and it was likely a pursuit had already begun. The north wind that prevented the *Pearl* from sailing up the bay would drive it southward down the Chesapeake, putting more distance between the schooner and any pursuers. According to Drayton, "I urged Sayres to go to sea, with the intention of reaching the Delaware by the outside passage. But he objected that the vessel was not fit to go outside (which was true enough) and that the bargain was to go to Frenchtown."[163] There was a third option that neither Drayton nor Sayres seemed to consider: sail the *Pearl* out of the Potomac and let the strong northly wind drive the schooner across the bay to near Virginia's Eastern Shore. There, they could anchor and wait for the wind to change. The Chesapeake was at its widest in that area, which would make it harder for any pursuers to find them. When the wind shifted, the *Pearl* could sail northward to Frenchtown, where help awaited the freedom seekers. Perhaps the reason that Drayton did not raise this possibility was that he did not know this part of the bay waters well. Perhaps his misfortunes were not a result of bad luck but bad seamanship.

According to their agreement, Sayres had the last word about where the *Pearl* sailed, and on Sunday evening, Drayton reluctantly anchored the schooner in Cornfield Harbor, a large crescent of calm water just west of Point Lookout and the entrance to Chesapeake Bay. With nothing left to do, Drayton and most of the others went to sleep.

On Sunday morning, affluent Washington residents were waking up from a night of torchlight parades and rousing speeches that celebrated the news of a revolution in Europe that threatened to usher in a wave of liberty across Europe. As the Washingtonians awoke, some discovered that their enslaved people were missing. Soon, neighbors reported that their enslaved, too, were gone, and it was soon obvious that something unusual was amiss. According to Drayton, "Great was the wonder at the sudden and simultaneous disappearance of so many 'prime hands,' roughly estimated, though probably with considerable exaggeration, as worth in the market not less than $100,000—and all at 'one fell swoop.'"[164]

As the news spread, a posse was gathered to hunt down the fugitives, and someone reported that a schooner had delivered a load of wood and mysteriously departed. One of the wealthy steamboat owners, who was missing three of his enslaved laborers, offered his vessel, the *Salem*, to purse the runaways.[165] While the steamboat made preparations to disembark, a gang of several dozen men, all boisterous, angry and armed, scrambled on board the *Salem*. Unhampered by considerations of wind, the steamboat plowed steadily southward down the Potomac, reaching the mouth of the river just before dawn. As the captain of the steamboat approached the Chesapeake Bay, he slowed the *Salem*. The boat did not carry insurance for cruising in bay waters, and he did not want to continue the pursuit any farther. As he turned the *Salem* around to return to Washington, someone noticed the dark shape of a schooner in Cornfield Cove. It was the *Pearl*.[166]

It was still dark on Monday morning when the freedom seekers were awakened by the sound of a steamboat blowing off steam, the thud of footsteps on the *Pearl's* deck and the shouts of angry men. Suddenly, the hatch was thrown open, and a loud voice announced, "N—rs, by God!"[167] As the runaways realized that their escape had failed, some shrieked, and others began to cry. The posse was armed with guns and clubs, and in the face of

A slave pen in Alexandria, Virginia, where freedom seekers from the *Pearl* may have been held. *Courtesy of the Library of Congress.*

overwhelming force, the freedom seekers were forced to surrender. Richard Edmondson led the group of freedom seekers out of the hold, exclaiming a line from St. Paul, which he said when he wanted to calm his prison guards, "Do yourself no harm, gentlemen, for we are all here!"[168]

Most of the posse's anger was directed toward Drayton and Sayres, and for a moment, it appeared that they would lynch the two white men on the spot. After the men were tied in pairs, the *Pearl* was secured to the *Salem*, and the mournful journey back up the Potomac to Washington began. Along the way, the fugitives ate some of the provisions and sang to relieve their sorrow.[169] When the two vessels reached the city, they were greeted by an angry mob, and as the freedom seekers disembarked, those in the crowd yelled curses and insults at them. One man with a knife lunged at Drayton and cut off a small part of his ear. As the runaways marched on their way to jail, one from the mob called out to Emily Edmondson, "Aren't you ashamed to run away and make all this trouble for everybody?" The teenager replied, "No sir, we are not, and if we had to go through it again, we'd do the same thing."[170]

Eventually, the wrath of the mob turned on the offices of the abolitionist newspaper the *National Era*, and the unrest lasted several days. By that time, the freedom seekers were shipped to slave dealers to be sold. The freedom seekers on the *Pearl*, including the Edmondson siblings, faced the indignities of the slave pens in Alexandria, Virginia, and the New Orleans slave auction market.

HARRIET TUBMAN'S QUEST FOR FREEDOM

By the time the mass escape of the freedom seekers on the *Pearl* failed, Minty Ross had been married to John Tubman for four years, and she was now known to her friends and relatives as Harriet Tubman.[171] Little is known of her married life, and although John was a free man, Harriet continued to work as an enslaved laborer. The diminutive Harriet developed into a skilled field hand who could handle the physically demanding jobs. She plowed fields, hauled timber, drove a team of oxen and did all the work performed by the male hands. In the nineteenth century, many of the fields along the banks of the rivers of the Eastern Shore were covered with forests whose timber was used to construct sloops, schooners and other sailing vessels in the towns near the Chesapeake Bay. Much of this timber was cut some distance from the riverbanks, and it had to be carted to a stream where it could be floated to nearby shipyards or loaded onto a vessel that would carry it to Baltimore or another large shipbuilding site. Harriet was able to strike a deal with her owner—similar to what Frederick Douglass did in Baltimore—to pay him a fixed annual sum in return for the freedom to hire herself out to other farmers and keep the excess money. Over time, she accumulated forty dollars and used it to purchase a yoke of oxen, which she used to hire herself out to other farmers to accumulate even more money.[172] Harriet, however, was not interested in money. As she moved from farm to farm, Tubman came upon other enslaved laborers who shared with her details of friendly houses and routes to the north. Especially helpful were the watermen who worked on the sailing vessels that carried the timber to Baltimore and other Chesapeake Bay ports. The Black sailors had a wealth of information about towns up and down the Chesapeake.[173] Sometimes, Tubman hired herself out to farmers in Caroline County, and she may have been living there in 1849, when her owner died. When her owner's estate was settled, his enslaved laborers were to be sold.[174] Years later, Tubman dictated her life's story to Sarah Bradford, the author of a number of children's books and biographies of Peter the Great of Russia and Christopher Columbus. Bradford wrote, "No one knew how it had come out, but someone had heard that Harriet and two of her

The Appoquinimink Meeting House may have been a station on the Underground Railroad. *Courtesy of the Delaware Public Archives.*

brothers were very soon—perhaps today, perhaps tomorrow—to be sent far South with a gang brought up for plantation work."[175] In the past, several of Tubman's siblings had already been sold away, and she was determined not to let it happen to her.[176]

Harriet talked to her husband, John, and told him that she was going to run away, but he was already a free man, and leaving his home in Dorchester County was not without risks. Although he had free papers, John would have to travel to an unfamiliar region where he could be stopped, questioned and forced to show his papers by any white man, who could proclaim the papers a forgery and refuse to return them. Such an encounter could result in John being sold back into slavery. On the other hand, as a free man, he could move about during the day, scout the route, ask questions about friendly farms, buy food and generally smooth the way for Harriet's escape. In the end, John declined to join Harriet in her escape effort, which led to an ever-widening fracture in their marriage.

Harriet then met with two of her brothers, Ben and Henry, and they decided to join her in her escape, but first, she went through the enslaved laborers' quarters singing, "When that old chariot comes, I'm going to leave you, I'm bound for the promised land," as a sign to the other enslaved people that she was about to leave. There was no moon shining on the Eastern Shore on September 17, 1849, when Harriet, with two of her brothers, boarded the Underground Railroad and headed to Delaware.

Two weeks later, their owner's widow placed an advertisement offering $300 for the capture and return of the three fugitives. The advertisement described Henry as "aged about 19 years, has on one side of his neck a wen, just under the ear, he is of dark chestnut color, about 5 feet, 8 or nine inches [in height]." Ben was "about 25 years [old], is very quick to speak when spoken to, he is of chestnut color, about six feet high; Minty, aged about 27 years, is of chestnut color, fine looking and about 5 feet high." The advertisement offered a reward of $100 each if they were taken out of state or $50 each if they were taken in Maryland. The advertisement asked if "the *Delaware Gazette* will please copy the above."[177]

After more than two weeks of trekking across Delmarva's unfamiliar countryside, hiding by day, traveling by night and scavenging food wherever they could find it, Tubman's two brothers began to regret running away. Tubman recalled, "[T]he way was strange, the north was far away, and all the unknown, the masters would purse and recapture them, and their fate would be worse than ever before; as so they broke away from her, and bidding her good-bye, they hastened back to the known horrors of slavery, and the dread that which was worse."[178] When her two brothers decided to return home, Harriet reluctantly followed them back to their owners.

Tubman learned several valuable lessons. She was determined to never again turn back once she started on the Underground Railroad. She also was determined to not let any of those she was leading turn back. Sometime in October, several weeks after her first scuttled attempt aboard the Underground Railroad, Tubman started out again, but this time, she traveled alone. A friendly white woman gave her two names of people who would assist her in her escape. The woman also gave Tubman directions to a safe house that served as an Underground Railroad station where she would find the first of the two people who would help her. When Tubman stopped at the safe house, she was helped to the second house. Tubman gave the white woman who helped her a quilt and journeyed toward Delaware. Tubman reasoned, "There was one of two things I had a right to: liberty or death; if I could not have one, I would have the other; for no man should take me alive; I should fight for my liberty as long as my strength lasted."[179] Tubman's exact route out of Maryland has not been determined, but there was a strong Quaker community living in Caroline County, and some of them actively supported the Underground Railroad. The people who assisted Harriet may have been members of the Marshy Creek Friends of the Northwest Fork Meeting.[180] When Tubman reached the first safe house, a woman asked her to sweep the front yard, a ruse to give Tubman's presence legitimacy. When

Right: Harriet Tubman just after the Civil War. *Courtesy of the Library of Congress*.

Below: The Little Creek Meeting House was purported to be an Underground Railroad station. *Courtesy of the Delaware Public Archives*.

the woman's husband returned home, he loaded his wagon, and Harriet hid in the wagon while the husband drove her to the next safe house.[181] At the second safe house, Tubman received directions to the next station on the Underground Railroad.

At this point, Tubman was close, if not over, the Delaware border with Maryland. Using the North Star as her guide, Tubman moved up the western edge of Delaware. On cloudy nights when the stars were not visible, she followed the streams and creeks that generally moved from north to south. This kept her west of the high ground that ran down the spine of the Delmarva Peninsula and separated the waters that flowed into the Chesapeake Bay from those that emptied into the Delaware Bay.

A formidable task that all freedom seekers from that part of the Delmarva Peninsula faced was crossing the Chesapeake and Delaware Canal. The waterway stretched across the peninsula about a dozen miles south of Wilmington and formed a barrier between Thomas Garrett's band of Underground Railroad agents and any fugitives who were hoping to make their way to Pennsylvania. The canal's waters were sixty-six feet wide and could be crossed by a swimmer of moderate ability.[182] Those who could not swim could use a log as a rudimentary raft and paddle their way across in a matter of minutes. Close to either end of the canal were locks, whose doors could provide nimble fugitives a footbridge over the canal, but they risked not only falling but also discovery by the lock's operators. In addition, there were several swing bridges along the canal's route, but they were not always in place for fugitives to cross the canal, and freedom seekers also risked discovery by the bridges' attendants. The easiest crossing was a 247-foot-long covered bridge at Summit near the middle of the canal. It is likely that Harriet learned about the canal from watermen with whom she dealt in her timber hauling work. Agents of the Underground Railroad south of the canal could have advised her of the best way to cross the waterway.

Harriet continued to make her way north and crossed the canal without any apparent difficulty. She was now close to Wilmington. Walking by night and hiding by day, she continued to make her way north. Not knowing who to trust, she used her intuition to ask strangers for food or to guide her on her way. Tubman apparently did not encounter Thomas Garrett or any of his operatives who would have eased her journey to the North. She may have passed between Newark and Wilmington to reach the northern Delaware border, where she crossed into the free state of Pennsylvania. Unable to read road signs, she may have been told that she was in Pennsylvania when she reached a distinctive building. When Tubman realized that she was in a free state, she believed that she would never again have to call anyone "master." Harriet recalled, "I looked at my hands to see if I was the same person now [that] I was free. There was such a glory over everything; the sun came like gold through the trees and over the fields, and I felt like I was in heaven."[183] She also realized the bitter truth that the rest of her family—her husband, parents, brothers and sister—were still enslaved in Maryland, and the failed escape of her two brothers showed that unless Harriet made an effort to go back to rescue them, they would be condemned to a life of slavery, and she would never see them again, nor would she know what happened to them. In that moment of freedom, Tubman resolved to make a home for them in the North and return to and lead them to freedom on the Delaware Underground Railroad.[184]

Frederick Douglass and Harriet Tubman became two towering figures of the Underground Railroad, and each in their own way were heroes of the abolitionist cause. Both lived not far from each other on Maryland's Eastern Shore; both failed on their first escape attempt, and both traveled through Delaware to freedom. Douglass, however, was literate, and he used his ability to read and write to effect his escape. Eventually, he became a talented speaker for the abolitionist cause. His three autobiographies are filled with acute observations about slavery and other topics and are outstanding examples of nineteenth-century literature. When Douglass made his escape from Baltimore, he was assisted by his free fiancée, Anna Murray, who later joined him in the North. When Douglass escaped, he rode comfortably on a train and a steamboat. The only time he was on foot was when he walked openly through downtown Wilmington to catch the steamboat for Philadelphia. Douglass's escape took less than a day. Although Douglass had relatives enslaved in Maryland, his owner's attempt to break family ties was successful, and Douglass gave little thought to returning to Maryland to rescue them. Tubman, on the other hand, never learned to read or write, which created numerous obstacles in her escape attempt. When she recounted her life story, she had to dictate it to a white woman, Sarah Bradford, who recorded her words in a heavy Eastern Shore accent. When she ran away from Maryland into Delaware, she had to cover nearly one hundred miles on foot, sleeping in the brush or other hiding places during the day, walking along darkened roads at night and scavenging for food wherever she could find it, not knowing whether she was following the right route or what dangers lie ahead. Her footsore journey to freedom took many days, and when she reached the free state of Pennsylvania, she was a "stranger in a strange land." Unlike Douglass, however, slavery did not break the bonds between Tubman and her family members. Once Tubman was free, she was determined, no matter the consequences, to return to Maryland to lead her relatives along the Delaware Underground Railroad.

THOMAS GARRETT'S PROPHECY

When Thomas Garrett addressed the court at the conclusion of his trial for harboring the Hawkins family, the Wilmington businessman declared that he would continue to assist freedom seekers. Garrett predicted, "The reports of these trials will be published by editors from Maine to Texas and the far west; and what must be the effect produced? It will no doubt add hundreds, perhaps thousands, to the present large and rapidly increasing army of abolitionists."[185] Garrett admitted that he and Hunn were immediately hurt by the court's verdict, but the Quaker businessman believed that the court's decision "will have a powerful effect in bringing about the abolition of slavery in this country, this land of boasted freedom, where only the slave is fettered at the south by his lordly master, but the white man at the north is bound as in chains to do the bidding of his southern masters."[186]

Garrett went on to explain the abolitionists belief that the federal constitution favored the slaveholding states. He declared, "I am *sorry* to have to admit this truth: that the slave states and slave interests have ruled the nation

Antislavery poster. *Courtesy of the Library of Congress.*

from the Declaration of Independence till the present time."[187] Although Garrett did not mention it in his speech, when counting a state's population to allocate seats in the House of Representatives, the Constitution provided a state's population "shall be determined by adding to the whole number of free persons…three-fifths of all other persons [slaves]."[188] In effect, southern representation was increased by three-fifths by the region's enslaved population, who could not vote and who had no role in choosing their representatives. In 1850, Connecticut, with a white population of 383,099, had four seats in the House of Representatives, but South Carolina, with a white population of 274,563, had six members in the House. South Carolina was given two extra seats in the House on the strength of the nearly 400,000 enslaved laborers within its borders who otherwise remained outside the political process. In the decade before the Civil War, the slave states had approximately twenty more members in the House of Representatives than they would have if the three-fifths rule were not in effect.

Garrett went on to point out that most of the U.S. presidents were from slave states. At the time he was speaking, all of the presidents, except for John Adams and his son, John Quincy Adams, from Massachusetts, had been slave owners. Martin Van Buren of New York owned a single enslaved person. George Washington, Thomas Jefferson, James Madison, James Monroe, Andrew Jackson, William Henry Harrison, John Tyler and James K. Polk all enslaved people. Garrett contended that not only were the overwhelming majority of U.S. presidents southern slave owners, but the majority of cabinet officers, foreign ministers and Supreme Court justices were also slave owners, and "they have made our laws to suit their *peculiar institutions*."[189]

Turning to the annexation of Texas in 1845, Garrett maintained, "Texas was admitted in a day with the dash of a pen, with her mixed and motley crew of inhabitants as good and loyal subjects of these United States; when at the same time…most foreigners coming amongst us and adopting this country as their future home must knock for years for admission as a citizen before they can be admitted. They must swear to support the Constitution and pay a fee for admission."[190]

Texas was admitted to the Union as a slave state, and with the unique authority to divide into five separate states, Garrett pointed out that "the admission of Texas was the cause of the Mexican War, where hundreds of millions of the peoples' money has been wasted and thousands of valuable lives sacrificed by sword and climate, all for the slave interest. No intelligent man doubts this fact; it was the slave interest, cruel, disgraceful and unrighteous war."[191] For over a decade, congressmen were forbidden to speak on the subject of slavery, but as Garrett maintained, "now it is the all-engrossing subject. It enters more or less into every subject brought before either house at Washington."

The attempted mass escape of freedom seekers on the *Pearl* occurred the month before Garrett's trial, and the incident resulted in a full-blown debate about slavery and the slave trade. According to Garrett, the debate "is what abolitionists have been laboring for.…Look at the nations around us. The

Left: Henry Clay, the Great Compromiser. *Courtesy of the Library of Congress.*

Below: Effects of the Fugitive Slave Act. *Courtesy of the Library of Congress.*

cause of freedom is progressing with railroad speed." Garrett was optimistic that the growing power of the antislavery movement in the North and West would overcome the constitutional advantages held by the South. If the South continued to maintain slavery in the face of the growing popularity of the abolitionist movement, Garrett predicted that "before ten years from this date, there will be a dissolution of the Union."[192]

Garrett was right that the United States was heading for "a dissolution of the Union," but he was wrong about the effects of a spirited debate about slavery. The Quaker businessman, like everyone else, was surprised by the discovery of gold in California later that year that initiated the gold rush of 1849. California very quickly clamored for admission to the Union, which would upset the balance between the slave and free states and threatened the southern hegemony in the Senate. With no apparent slave territory ready for admission, Congress looked for another way to forge a compromise. An aged Henry Clay, who drafted the Missouri Compromise in 1820, was able to broker a deal that included a series of laws that collectively became known as the Compromise of 1850. Among other things, California was admitted as a free state, and the slave trade was prohibited in Washington, D.C., a goal the backers of the *Pearl* enterprise sought. To appease the southerners, the compromise included a strong Fugitive Slave Act that gave federal marshals the authority to "execute all warrants and precepts issued under the provisions of this act," which took the handling of freedom seekers out of the hands of local authorities. The Fugitive Slave Law of 1850 also negated the personal liberty laws that helped shield fugitives from the slave catchers. The new law empowered federal marshals to call any bystanders to aid them, and "all good citizens are hereby commanded to aid and assist the prompt and efficient execution of this law, whenever their services may be required." The owners of runaways were empowered to seize freedom seekers, and "in no trial or hearing under this act shall the testimony of such alleged furtive be admitted in evidence." The law also stated that "any person who shall knowingly and willingly obstruct, hinder or prevent" freedom seekers from being captured was committing a crime.

Thomas Garrett and other abolitionists had long sought a Congressional debate on the issue of slavery. They were appalled, however, when the debate led to the passage of a new Fugitive Slave Law, which made a violation of federal law many of the practices of the Underground Railroad. Thomas Garrett and others who were "willing obstruct, hinder or prevent" the apprehension of freedom seekers could be arrested under the new law. William Still, who had begun to keep records of the runaways he assisted, destroyed those records for fear of implicating agents of the Underground Railroad. Slave catchers could enlist federal marshals to assist them, and recognizing that slave catchers and kidnappers were not encumbered by state laws, slave owners were emboldened to pursue and capture any Black American, secure in the knowledge that any claim by a Black person that they had apprehended the wrong person or that they were free was not admissible in court.

After the Fugitive Slave Law of 1850 became law, slave owners renewed their efforts to recover what they considered their lost property. Across the North, abolitionists railed against the "slaveocracy" that the United States had become, and Harriet Beecher Stowe was moved to write *Uncle Tom's Cabin*, which included the character Simeon Halliday, who was modeled after Thomas Garrett. The character was described as "a tall, straight, muscular man in drab coat and pantaloons, and broad-brimmed hat."[193] When Harriet Tubman returned to Maryland to facilitate the escape of her relatives and others, the new Fugitive Slave Law presented her with new dangers as she conducted freedom seekers along the Delaware Underground Railroad. Just north of the Mason-Dixon line in Pennsylvania, the formerly enslaved people who were living as free people were in particular danger, as slave owners and kidnappers from Maryland and Delaware sought to retrieve those who were once their enslaved laborers. The former fugitives, however, were intelligent, organized and armed. They would not return to slavery without a fight.

HARRIET TUBMAN RESCUES KIZZY

When Harriet Tubman first reached Pennsylvania in the fall of 1849, she may have been "a stranger in a strange land," but she did not remain that way for long. She made her way to Philadelphia, where she was embraced by the large free Black community and their abolitionist friends. For the first time in her life, she could move about freely without asking for the approval of her owner. She found work as housekeeper, which could be demanding work, but it was nothing compared to driving oxen, hauling wood and plowing fields. Although Pennsylvania was a free state, Tubman still had to be leery of slave catchers who combed the Black community in Philadelphia for runaways. In the year that Tubman escaped, she was one of 259 documented freedom seekers who fled from Maryland.[194] Like Tubman, many of these fugitives made their way to Philadelphia, and they were followed by professional slave

Harriet Tubman in the 1880s. *Courtesy of the Library of Congress.*

catchers who earned tidy sums by rounding up suspicious Black people in the City of Brotherly Love.

In December 1850, after the Fugitive Slave Law had been passed and over a year after Tubman had left Maryland, she learned that her niece Kessiah Bowley, sometimes called "Kizzy," and her two children were about to be auctioned off.[195] Kessiah was married to John Bowley, a free Black waterman. How Harriet learned about the impending sale is not known, but it demonstrates the robust communication network that existed among the Black community in the Delaware-Maryland region. Tubman frequently dealt with watermen who transported her lumber to Baltimore, and she likely expanded her contacts among the sailors of the Philadelphia waterfront. They may have carried a message, either written or verbal, to her relatives in Maryland. However it was done, Harriet learned that Kessiah and her children were be sold, and Tubman was determined to rescue them.

Traveling back into a slave state like Maryland was risky, and to return to Cambridge on the Eastern Shore, where she might be recognized for the auction, was too dangerous for her to risk. Tubman probably had freedom papers or, at the very least, a traveling pass forged for her in case she was questioned. In addition, Black people who traveled south from Philadelphia to Baltimore drew less attention than Black people traveling north. At any rate, Tubman boarded a train or a steamboat bound for Baltimore. When Frederick Douglass made his escape in 1838, the tracks stopped at Wilmington, and he had to take a steamboat from the Delaware town to Philadelphia. In 1851, if Tubman took the train to Baltimore, her trip through the northern neck of Delaware would have taken less than an hour. Railroad passengers traveling between Philadelphia and Baltimore still had to disembark at the Susquehanna River in Maryland, where a railroad bridge across the river had not yet been built. She also could have taken a steamboat. In 1844, the Baltimore and Philadelphia Steamboat Company established regular service between the two cities via the Chesapeake and Delaware Canal. The company used narrow shallow-draft vessels that were designed to fit through the one-hundred-by-twenty-two-foot locks of the canal.[196] Unlike the paddle-wheelers that were common on western rivers, the Baltimore and Philadelphia Steamboat Company's vessels were driven by Ericsson screw propellers, and the company touted itself as the Ericsson Line.[197]

Tubman reached Baltimore without incident, and she was able to stay with her brother-in-law, Tom Tubman, a stevedore who may have lived in Fell's Point, the former neighborhood of Frederick Douglass. On the day of

Narrow steamboat in the Chesapeake and Delaware Canal. *Courtesy of the Delaware Public Archives.*

the auction, Harriet remained in Baltimore, while the auction of Kessiah and her children took place across the Chesapeake Bay in Cambridge, the county seat of Dorchester County. A little before lunchtime, a crowd gathered around the courthouse, and Kessiah and her children were brought to the courthouse steps to be inspected so the bidding could begin. One of the most spirited bidders was an unrecognized Black man, and he had the winning bid.

With the sale seemingly completed, the auctioneer decided to break for lunch. When everyone was finished eating and the auction was set to resume, it was found that Kessiah and her children had disappeared. The mysterious Black bidder was John Bowley, Kessiah's husband. While the auctioneer and most of the onlookers were at lunch, Bowley slipped away with his wife and children to a safe house just five minutes from the courthouse. When the auctioneer returned and discovered that Kessiah and her children were missing, he declared the sale was void, and he continued to auction off other enslaved people.[198]

After night had fallen, Bowley led his family to a small log canoe that was moored on the Choptank River, just outside of town. Log canoes were descended from the Native canoes that were constructed by hollowing out logs using fire and stone implements. A log canoe was made by shaping and fastening up to seven logs together and adding two sharply raked masts for sails. The resulting undecked vessel could be up to forty feet long, and it rode low on the water, exposing those aboard to the frigid December bay waters. Most log canoes were used by oystermen who tonged the bivalves from the bay's bottom and brought them directly aboard the low-riding vessel. Log canoes were fast, and watermen delighted in racing them to see whose was the fastest.[199] After the Bowley family boarded John's log canoe, they set sail across the bay with the cold bay waters splashing about them, and they reached Baltimore safely.

After waiting for a few days to recover from the auction and the harrowing trip across the bay, Harriet led them north. By this time, she was familiar with the Underground Railroad routes through Delaware and into Philadelphia. It is not known whether she and the Bowley family took the train or a steamboat, but it is known that they reached the Pennsylvania city safely. Tubman had completed her first foray back into slave territory. It would not be, by any means, her last trip into a slave state.[200]

HARRIET TUBMAN, FREDERICK DOUGLASS AND SOME SYSTEM ABOUT THIS BUSINESS

Several months after Harriet Tubman had orchestrated the escape of Kessiah and her two children, Harriet returned to Baltimore to lead her brother Moses and two others to freedom. Not much is known about this incident, but it appears that Tubman may have traveled to Baltimore by steamboat from Philadelphia, through the Chesapeake and Delaware Canal and southward on the Chesapeake Bay to the Maryland city. The fact that she retraced the route she used in Kizziah's escape suggests that she may have befriended someone on one of the steamboats plying the Philadelphia-Baltimore route.[201]

Toward the end of 1851, Tubman made yet another trip to Maryland, but this time, she returned to her former home in Dorchester County on the Eastern Shore. She may have left Philadelphia again by boat, but it has been suggested that she traveled by land through Delaware. Harriet had been away for two years, and she wanted to be reunited with her husband, John. She bought him a new suit of clothes to celebrate their reunion, but when she reached Dorchester County, she discovered that he had remarried. His new wife was a free woman, and John refused to leave her for Harriet.[202] Deeply disappointed, years later, she told her biographer, "She did not give way to rage or grief but collected a party of fugitives and brought them safely to Philadelphia."[203] Her anger passed, and she quickly returned to the work of leading enslaved people to freedom. In the Black community of Dorchester County and the surrounding area, news of her success in leading Kizzy and others to freedom had begun to spread. Enslaved people outside of her family circle were eager to join her to escape bondage. In December, she returned to Maryland yet again and, perhaps jolted by John's rejection of her, began to conduct non–family members along the Underground Railroad through Delaware. On this occasion, she led out eleven freedom seekers; among them were another one of her brothers, William Henry, and his wife.[204]

Years later, Tubman recalled that sometimes, members of her party would become exhausted and declare they could not go on. They would drop down to the ground, declaring that they would sooner die where they were than go any farther. Others said that a voluntary return to slavery would be better than being overtaken by their pursuers. Tubman knew that any freedom seekers who went back or were caught would be subjected to brutal whippings and other tortures to make them reveal the route they took though Delaware. Any fugitive who had traveled just a small part of the Delaware Underground Railroad could expose the names and locations of the safe houses on the trail to Wilmington. Tubman carried a revolver to prevent anyone from leaving her care. She said, "Go on or die," and she professed that dead men tell no tales.[205] With the enactment of the Fugitive Slave Law in 1850, many freedom seekers did not feel safe in Pennsylvania; therefore, Tubman led her party of eleven to Canada, and this may have led her directly to Frederick Douglass.[206]

In addition to speaking and writing against the evils of slavery, another important aspect of Frederick Douglass's antislavery work was harboring groups of fugitives in his home in Rochester, New York, on the south shore of Lake Ontario. He later wrote, "[M]y prominence as an abolitionist… naturally made me the stationmaster and conductor of the underground railroad passing through this goodly city." Douglass also recalled, "Secrecy and concealment were necessary conditions to the successful operation of this railroad and hence its prefix *underground*."[207] After Douglass released his first autobiography in the 1840s, he admitted to being an escaped enslaved laborer, and his national reputation made him liable to arrest. Douglass wrote, "I could take no step in it without exposing myself to fine and imprisonment, for these were the penalties imposed by the fugitive slave law for feeding, harboring, or otherwise assisting a slave to escape from his master; but, in face of this fact, I can say I never did more congenial,

Niagara Falls Bridge, the last link in the Underground Railroad. *Courtesy of the Library of Congress.*

attractive, fascinating, and satisfactory work." In the 1850s, there were nearly four million enslaved people in the United States, but a very small fraction of these people escaped bondage on the Underground Railroad. Nevertheless, Douglass wrote, "[I]t was like an attempt to bail out the ocean with a teaspoon, but the thought that there was one less slave and one more freeman, having myself been a slave and a fugitive slave—brought to my heart unspeakable joy."[208] On one occasion, Douglass recalled hosting a party of eleven enslaved people who remained with him until he gathered enough money to transport them on the last leg of their journey to Canada. Some historians theorize that this was the group of eleven whom Harriet Tubman led out of Maryland through Delaware and Pennsylvania. Once in Pennsylvania, they took the train to Rochester and eventually Canada. It is not known when Tubman and Douglass first met. It is even possible that they first crossed paths while they were still held in bondage in Maryland. By the early 1850s, Douglass was nationally known, and Tubman's work was becoming known in abolitionist circles, but it otherwise remained a secret.

In 1868, three years after the Civil War ended, Tubman, who was illiterate, dictated her life's story to Sarah Bradford. Before Bradford's work was published, Tubman wrote to Douglass for a letter recommending the book. He used the occasion to contrast his work on the Underground

Railroad with Tubman's. Douglass wrote, "You ask for what you do not need when you call upon me for a word of commendation. I need such words from you far more than you can need them from me, especially where your superior labors and devotion to the cause of the lately enslaved of our land are known as I know them."[209] Reflecting on the different roles they played in the Underground Railroad, Douglass continued:

> *Most that I have done and suffered in the service of our cause has been in public, and I have received much encouragement at every step of the way. You, on the other hand, have labored in a private way. I have wrought in the day—you in the night. I have had the applause of the crowd and the satisfaction that comes of being approved by the multitude, while the most that you have done has been witnessed by a few trembling, scarred, and foot-sore bondmen and women, whom you have led out of the house of bondage, and whose heartfelt, 'God bless you,' has been your only reward.*[210]

Douglass continued, "The midnight sky and the silent stars have been the witnesses of your devotion to freedom and of your heroism. Excepting John Brown—of sacred memory—I know of no one who has willingly encountered more perils and hardships to serve our enslaved people than you have."[211]

Fugitives from the Eastern Shore were led by Harriet Tubman through Delaware. *From Still, Underground Rail Road.*

The number of freedom seekers compared to the total number of people held in bondage was small, but fugitives who successfully made their way to freedom served as an inspiration for others to board the Underground Railroad, and the increased number of runaways did not go unnoticed by the slave owners of the Eastern Shore. On August 14, 1849, the Talbot County newspaper, the *Easton Star*, complained, "Almost every week, we hear one or more slaves making their escape, and if something is not speedily done to put a stop to it, that kind of property will hardly be worth owning. There seems to be some system about this business, and we strongly suspect they are assisted in their escape by organized bands of abolitionists." The newspaper was blinded by the unfounded belief that most enslaved people were happy, and they thought the enslaved incapable of conceiving a plan to run away. Although many of the freedom seekers were assisted by Quaker agents of the Underground Railroad in Maryland and Delaware, the escape was almost always initiated by the freedom seeker. The *Easton Star* went on to suggest that a telegraph line be constructed along the length of the Delmarva Peninsula and that a series of slave catchers be stationed along the line so that word could be spread quickly of any enslaved people who were reported missing. The exasperated newspaper editors lamented, "At present, all efforts to recover them after they once made their escape appears fruitless."[212] Little did the slave owners of the Eastern Shore know that an unassuming, twenty-something woman whom they knew as Minty was generating "some system about this business."

VIOLENCE ON THE TRACK

Should a slave, when assault[ed], *but raise his hand in self-defense, the white assaulting party is fully justified by southern, or Maryland public opinion, in shooting the slave down.*
—*Fredrick Douglass*[213]

The Fugitive Slave Law

Euphemia Williams was born in Pennsylvania in the early nineteenth century, and under the terms of the state's gradual abolition law, she was free. By 1851, the year after the Fugitive Slave Law was passed, she was married and had six children. Her oldest child was a teenager, and the youngest was an infant. At dawn on February 6, Euphemia was peacefully sleeping with her children in their Philadelphia home near the corner of Fifth Street and Germantown Road. Suddenly, several men burst into the house, grabbed Williams and began to haul her away. One of her teenage daughters cried out, "They've got my mother! They've got my mother!" As the men hustled Williams out of the house, Euphemia shouted, "For God's sake, save me!" Alerted by the commotion, several of Euphemia's neighbors ran into the street, but they could not prevent the woman from being carried off to the marshal's office, where she was charged with being Mahala Purnell, who had run away from her owner in Maryland twenty-two years earlier.[214]

In the 1820s, Mahala was held in bondage by Dr. George W. Purnell of Worcester County, Maryland, which bordered Sussex County, Delaware. In

1827, Dr. Purnell hired Mahala out to Robert Bowen as a house servant, and when Bowen was away at a camp meeting, Mahala ran away, left Maryland and traveled northward on the budding Delaware Underground Railroad. Bowen later claimed that he and Dr. Purnell advertised in Georgetown, Milford and Millsboro for the capture of Mahala. Bowen and Purnell, however, lost track of the freedom seeker at Delaware City, near the eastern entrance to the Chesapeake and Delaware Canal.

Dr. Purnell died in 1844, and ownership of Mahala passed to William T.J. Purnell, one of Dr. Purnell's sons. When the Fugitive Slave Law was passed, over two decades after Mahala ran away, Robert Bowen and William Purnell seized the opportunity to recapture their enslaved laborer. Purnell, Bowen and some others went to Philadelphia to look for Mahala, and amazingly, Bowen spotted someone who he claimed was Mahala in a house at the corner of Fifth Street and Germantown Roads. The woman was not Mahala. She was Euphemia Williams. The Maryland kidnappers broke into the home and forcibly dragged Williams away to await a hearing that was to be held the next day.

Before the hearing began, a large number of alarmed white and Black residents crowded into the courtroom. Judge John K. Kane announced that the people in the room must be seated and that no one would be allowed to stand. The judge's order to limit the number of people who could witness the hearing in person likely prevented what could have been a chaotic situation.

After spectators, several lawyers for each side and Euphemia Williams, who was surrounded by her six children, were seated, Judge Kane gaveled the start of the proceedings. The opening witness, an overseer on Bowen's Maryland farm, set the tone for the prosecution when he testified, "I last saw her [Mahala] in 1827; she was about sixteen or seventeen; she was about an ordinary size, not the smallest size, nor the largest; she was neither thick nor thin; there was nothing remarkable in her than is common; nothing in her speech; she as about the same color as the woman here; I never saw a great deal of change in a n——r, from sixteen to thirty five or forty; sometimes they grew fatter and sometimes leaner." The overseer went on, "I knew her by her general favor [manner], and [she had] no particular mark; I would not attempt to describe features; her favor is familiar to me; I never saw any marks upon her."[215] Another witness for the claimants, J.T. Hammond, admitted he had never seen Mahala until he arrived at the courthouse, but he was ready to swear that he would have known her by her resemblance to Purnell's set of enslaved laborers. A lawyer for Euphemia asked, "His whole set?" "Yes, sir," Hammond replied, setting off a ripple of derisive laughter in the courtroom.[216] Other witnesses told similar stories, describing Mahala as plain and average-looking with no distinguishing characterizes or marks. Confident that the word of white witnesses, no matter how vague, would carry the case, the prosecution declined to present any documentary evidence, such as copies of the newspaper notices or handbills describing Mahala when she left Bowen's farm.

The lawyers defending Euphemia Williams steadfastly maintained that she was not Mahala Purnell. Her lawyers called several witnesses who testified that Euphemia was living in Pennsylvania at the time that Mahala was supposed to have run away from Purnell. The defense then called a Black woman named Sarah Gayly, who was about the same age as Euphemia. According to Gayly, "I have not seen her since 1826 until I saw her here in the courtroom; I recognized her when I first saw her here without anybody pointing her out, and she recognized me."[217]

Gayly testified that they played together as children, and she testified, "I have reason to know her, because she has the same sort of scar on her forehead that I have; we used to make fun of each other about the marks." Judge Kane asked Gayley and Williams to come forward so he could see the scars on the witness's forehead and that on Euphemia.[218] After the two women neared the judge, Euphemia removed her headscarf, and Judge Kane inspected the foreheads of the two women. He clearly saw similar scars on each of their foreheads and immediately dismissed the case.

When news of the decision spread to the people crowded outside, they erupted into loud cheers. Williams and her children were hurried into a carriage, which was driven through streets lined with ecstatic crowds. The horses were unhitched and replaced by a long rope, and as many Black people as could get hold of it pulled Williams and her children to their home.[219]

The case of Euphemia Williams was reported in newspapers from New York to New Orleans, and it demonstrated the incredible reach of the Fugitive Slave Law. Euphemia was fortunate that she was apprehended in Philadelphia, where a large Black community, able lawyers and a sympathetic judge enabled her to win her freedom. How many free Black Americans were kidnapped on lonely roads and taken to the South, where sympathy for people of color was in short supply?

Frederick Douglass summed up the reality of the Fugitive Slave Law:

The colored man's rights are less than those of a jackass. No man can take away a jackass without submitting the matter to twelve men in any part of this country. A black man may be carried away without any reference to a jury. It is only necessary to claim him, and that some villain should swear to his identity. There is more protection there for a horse, for a donkey or anything, rather than a colored man—who is, therefore, justified in the eye of God, in maintaining his right with his arm.[220]

Later in 1851, another case tested the reach of the Fugitive Slave Law with far different results. Like the men who pursued Mahala Purnell, Edward was determined to get his enslaved laborers back. On November 6, 1849, four men held in bondage at Gorsuch's farm in Baltimore County left and went northward on York Road to Christiana, Pennsylvania.[221] There, they met William Parker, an escaped enslaved man from Maryland. A tall, thin and muscular man in his late twenties, Parker was an imposing figure, and he was regarded as the leader and protector of the free Black community around Christiana.[222] Park helped the four freedom seekers settle into the Black community. Two years later, after the Fugitive Slave Law was passed, Edward Gorsuch saw a chance to retrieve his lost enslaved laborers.

In the late summer of 1851, Gorsuch learned that his four former enslaved laborers were living near Christiana in Lancaster County, Pennsylvania, and he gathered a posse of a half-dozen relatives and others to travel to Pennsylvania to capture the freedom seekers. Gorsuch was familiar with the Fugitive Slave Law, and he traveled by train to Philadelphia, obtaining the necessary warrants and the assistance of Deputy Marshal Henry H. Kline, known in the Black community as an infamous slave catcher.[223] While in Philadelphia, Kline attracted the attention of William Still and the Pennsylvania Anti-Slavery Society. By the 1850s, Still, Thomas Garrett and others had developed a network of contacts who alerted them to any unusual activity that might endanger freedom seekers. Still learned that Deputy Marshal Kline was going to Christiana to arrest a group of escaped enslaved people. Still enlisted the aid of Samuel Williams, a Black tavern owner and a former resident of Christiana, to follow Kline. Both Kline and Williams took the train from Philadelphia to Christiana, where Kline rendezvoused with Gorsuch and the other slave catchers. Williams went to warn Parker and other Black people living in the area.[224]

Parker alerted the four men who had escaped from Gorsuch's farm and got two of them into his house, a building with stone, fort-like walls. On September 11, 1851, Gorsuch, Kline and the half-dozen men of the posse arrived at the lane leading to Parker's house. Meanwhile, those inside, armed with a variety of firearms and long-handled farm tools, gathered on the second floor. One of the men from inside the building slipped out of the house and spotted Kline's posse. He immediately ran back to the house and cried, "O William! Kidnappers, kidnappers!"[225]

As some of the posse took positions on the four corners of the house to prevent anyone from escaping, Marshal Kline and slave owner Gorsuch approached the house and stepped inside. They found the first floor empty. Stopping at the bottom of a narrow staircase that led to the second floor, Kline announced that he had come to arrest the fugitives, and the marshal began to read the warrants for their arrest.[226] A standoff followed, with Gorsuch demanding the return of his "property" and those on the second-floor shouting threats to those who dared to come up the stairs. Eventually, someone threw a piece of metal, perhaps one of the farm implements, down the staircase, and Gorsuch and Kline retreated to the outside of the house, where the negotiations continued between the Black people on the second story and Kline and Gorsuch.[227]

The argument was interrupted by the sound of a horn coming from a window on the upper floor of the house. After several blasts, members of the posse silenced the horn by opening fire on the second-story window.[228] Shortly after the horn was sounded, two white men, Castner Hanway and Elijah Lewis, both Quakers who lived nearby, appeared on the pathway to the house. Almost immediately after the two white men arrived, a number of Black people, some alone and others in small groups, along with a few white residents, emerged from the woods and crossed the fields around the stone house.[229] Appearing like the minutemen gathering on Lexington Green at the start of the American Revolution, the men carried a variety of firearms, scythes and other farm tools that could be used as weapons. As the number approaching the house grew to over seventy-five or more men, Kline and his posse saw they were clearly outnumbered. Gorsuch, however, had not lost his determination to retrieve what he considered his rightful property.

During the protracted standoff, a metal farm tool and a wooden club were thrown from the second-story window, hitting two members of the posse, but the impasse continued.[230] Those on the second floor of the house came down to the first floor and crowded the doorway, where Gorsuch was demanding that the runaways come with him back to Maryland. One of the fugitives pistol-whipped Gorsuch, who was knocked down. Others opened fire on the prone Gorsuch, and some began to beat him with farm tools.[231] As Gorsuch lay dying, his son Dickinson rushed to aid his father, but he was hit by a shotgun blast and collapsed. With Marshal Kline running wildly through a cornfield, the rest of the outnumbered posse beat a hasty retreat.[232] The firing stopped. Edward Gorsuch was dead, and his son Dickinson had seventy shotgun pellets in his right side, but he survived. Others on both sides had received a variety of wounds, but none were serious.[233] What became known as the Christiana Riot was over.

William Parker and several Black Americans realized that the white authorities would not allow the killing of Gorsuch and the defeat of the slave catching posse to go unnoticed. Black Pennsylvania residents, free or fugitive, felt the state was no longer safe, and many Black Americans fled to the safety of Canada.[234] A contingent of United States Marines arrived in Christiana and arrested several dozen Black people who were suspected of participating in the riot.[235] All of those arrested were taken to Philadelphia.[236] Hanway and Lewis, whose appearance coincided with the arrival of the armed men, were taken prisoner and accused of being the ringleaders of the Black fighters. Slavery sympathizers could not believe that Black people could have organized such a well-coordinated resistance, and they blamed the two white men. Slaveholders also believed that the Black people present were not just defending the freedom seekers, but they saw it as an armed insurrection against the United States. With this, all the prisoners were charged with treason, a federal and a hanging offense.[237]

Associate justice of the Supreme Court Robert C. Grier and District Judge John K. Kane, who had heard the case of Euphemia Williams, presided

At the Christiana Riot, fugitives fought for their freedom. *From Still,* Underground Rail Road.

over the first trial, that of Castner Hanway.[238] Both judges declared they would uphold the Fugitive Slave Law, but in his charge to the jury, Judge Grier said there was no proof Hanway had conspired to make a general insurrection against the United States; there was no evidence presented that the defendant knew of the Fugitive Slave Law; and the rioters appeared to have no intention other than to protect one another. The jury deliberated for less than fifteen minutes and found Hanway not guilty. Although the State of Pennsylvania could have charged those responsible for the murder of Edward Gorsuch, so many participants had fled the area that no other indictments were brought. Like the Williams case, the Christiana Riot was reported nationwide as a sign that enforcement of the Fugitive Slave Law was not without its hazards. A year after the riot, Frederick Douglass said, "The only way to make the Fugitive Slave Law a dead letter is to make half a dozen or more dead kidnappers. A half dozen more dead kidnappers carried down South would cool the ardor of southern gentlemen and keep their rapacity in check."[239]

HARRIET TUBMAN RETURNS FOR HER BROTHERS

"Read my letter to the old folks, and give my love to them, and tell my brothers to be always watching unto prayer," one of the postal inspectors read aloud, "and when the good old ship Zion comes along, to be ready to step aboard." The letter was signed, "William Henry Jackson." Seeing nothing incriminating, the inspectors gave the letter to Jacob Jackson, the father of William Henry. Without so much as a glance, Jacob tossed it away, and he announced, "That letter can't be for me, no how. I can't make head nor tail of it." With that, Jackson left the post office.[240]

In December 1854, Jacob Jackson, a free Black man who lived in the Bucktown area of Dorchester County, was literate, and from time to time, he received letters from the North. The white residents from the part of the county suspected Jackson of being involved with the disappearance of a number of enslaved people, and when a letter arrived addressed to Jacob Jackson, the missive was opened by the inspectors to see if it implicated Jackson in the escape of any of the runaway enslaved laborers. Their suspicions were well-founded. Jackson had a son, William Henry Jackson (the name of the man who supposedly signed the letter) who had moved to the North. The letter meant nothing to the postal inspectors, and despite what he said to the inspectors, it meant a lot to Jacob Jackson. After he left the post office, he immediately went to alert three of Harriet Tubman's brothers, Benjamin, Robert and Henry, that Moses was coming to lead them to the promised land.[241]

Benjamin, twenty-eight, was owned by a woman who was "very devilish" and who required him to work hard for meager meals to support her "in idleness and luxury."[242] Robert, twenty-two, had been treated poorly, and "his feelings were those of an individual who had been unjustly in prison for a dozen years and had at last regained his liberty."[243] Henry (sometimes called John) Ross, twenty-two, was the father of two young sons, and his wife, Mary, was expecting a third child any day.[244] The three Ross brothers had attempted to escape earlier that year, and they believed that they would be sold just after the Christmas holiday.

After Jacob Jackson left the post office, he immediately went to Harriet's three brothers to tell them that they needed to be ready to leave at a moment's notice.[245] The increased danger posed by the Fugitive Slave Law did not deter Harriet Tubman from returning to Maryland to rescue her siblings and other freedom seekers. Although she sometimes traveled by steamboat or train, she most often retraced her steps along the Delaware Underground Railroad to Maryland. By now she knew the landmarks and sympathetic residents along the route, and that enabled her to make the trip relatively quickly.

Traveling into the slave states of Delaware and Maryland meant she risked capture, and if it was discovered that she was the one leading the exodus of fugitives, she could be sold to the Deep South for a lifetime sentence of hard labor or an immediate sentence of lynching. Although she possessed the knowledge, stamina and determination to free her remaining family members, she sometimes lacked the money to buy food or other resources she needed for an expedition to freedom. During the time between these forays, Tubman worked as a housekeeper or cook to earn the money she needed to finance these trips. In the summer of 1852, she worked as a cook in Cape May, New Jersey, which was a growing seaside resort.[246] Cape May was also a center for abolitionist activity in southern New Jersey.[247] Although records of Tubman's activities are sketchy, she may have contacted the abolitionists in the resort and some of the watermen who were instrumental in ferrying freedom seekers across the Delaware Bay to the free state of New Jersey. During this time, she became acquainted with William Still of the Pennsylvania Anti-Slavery Society and Thomas Garrett, the de facto Wilmington stationmaster of the Delaware Underground Railroad.

In December 1854, Tubman devised a plan to rescue three of her brothers who had attempted to escape before but were recaptured. Their attempts to run away motivated their masters to sell them, and the brothers feared that they would be sold south "to go down to the cotton and rice fields with the chain gang[s]."[248] Enslaved people were generally excused from working on Sundays and Christmas. In 1854, Christmas was on a Monday, and that meant there were two consecutive days that her brothers were not expected to work, and they would not be missed until Tuesday morning. Getting a two-day head start would enable the freedom seekers to be well into Delaware before they were missed. Tubman could neither read nor write, and she dictated her letter to Jacob Jackson to a literate friend. Harriet arrived near Bucktown on the Saturday before Christmas, and she sent word to her brothers that they would leave that night, but when they gathered to start their escape, Henry was missing. Tubman waited for no one. She led her two remaining brothers to her parents' house, about twenty miles northeast of Bucktown on Popular Neck in southern Caroline County, Maryland. During the day, they hid in a shed that kept corn and other fodder for the animals. The Ross brothers were joined by three other freedom seekers (two men and a woman) and their brother Henry. He had missed the first rendezvous because his wife was in labor, but after the baby was born, Henry faced the prospect of leaving his wife, their two sons and their newborn girl. Believing that he might be sold after Christmas, Henry and his wife agreed that it would be better for him to go without his family. If he made it to the North, he might be able to come back to rescue the rest of his family.[249]

While hiding in the fodder shed all day Sunday, Tubman's father, Ben Ross, brought them food and other supplies for their trip. Harriet and her brothers did not say goodbye to their mother, Rit, because they thought she would make such a scene that it would alert others that something unusual was happening. After darkness fell on Sunday, Christmas Eve, Tubman led the seven fugitives from her parents' home toward Delaware.

On Tuesday, the sale of the three Ross brothers was scheduled to begin, but they were nowhere to be found. Rit and Ben, their parents, denied seeing them over the holiday, and by this time, Tubman and her charges were deep into Delaware. It is not known what specific route the freedom seekers took. Harriet's band of fugitives could have continued some distance north before crossing into Delaware. Keeping the North Star on her left, she may have traveled east to Federalsburg, Maryland. From there, she and her party could have maintained an easterly course that led them into Delaware.[250] Near Bridgeville, she could have led the freedom seekers farther east until she encountered the major north–south road that ran from southern Delaware to Wilmington. Along this route, there were Underground Railroad stations at Milford, Frederica, Camden, Dover, Smyrna, Blackbird and Middletown. Some of these stations were only a few miles apart, and the freedom seekers may not have used them all on this escape. Whatever route they took, Tubman's party of freedom seekers had to cross the Chesapeake and Delaware Canal, and there was a station in Delaware City at the eastern terminus of the canal. The Underground Railroad agents there may have helped the fugitives cross the narrow waterway. After a stop at New Castle, it was only a half-dozen miles to Wilmington, where Tubman's group reached Thomas Garrett's house.[251] They had completed the approximately ninety-five-mile-long journey in four days.

Garrett welcomed the freedom seekers, and the next day, he wrote to an official of the Pennsylvania Anti-Slavery Society, "Esteemed Friend, J. Miller McKim: We made arrangements last night and sent away Harriet Tubman with six men and one woman to Allen Agnew's to be forwarded across the country to the city. Harriet and one of the men had worn their shoes off their feet, and I gave them two dollars to help fit them out and directed a carriage to be hired at my expense to take them out."[252]

Tubman and her party reached the Philadelphia office of the antislavery society without incident, and with the society's help, Tubman's group traveled on the aboveground railroad to St. Catharines, Canada, where there was a substantial Black population of formerly enslaved people.[253] Still used the record of their arrival to describe Tubman's importance and the methods she used on the Delaware Underground Railroad. Calling Tubman the Moses of the freedom seekers, Still wrote, "She had faithfully gone down into Egypt and had delivered these six bondsmen by her own heroism.…Yet, in point of courage, shrewdness and disinterested exertions to rescue her fellow men, by making personal visits to Maryland among the slaves, she was without her equal." Among the nearly one thousand freedom seekers Still interviewed, few professed a desire to return to the South to lead friends or relatives to the North. Still, however, wrote, "Time and again, she made successful visits to Maryland on the Underground Rail Road.…The idea of being captured by slave hunters or slaveholders seemed never to enter her mind." Tubman did not seem to care about her personal safety, but according to Still, she "was much more watchful with regard to those she was piloting." While on the road, Still maintained that "she would not suffer one of her party to whimper once about 'giving out and going back.'" According to Still, "Her like it is probable was never known before or since."[254]

Harriet Tubman: In Broad Daylight

An attractive young woman with light skin was held in bondage on a Maryland plantation by her mistress as a maid and dressmaker. Her name was Tilly. She was engaged to a young man who lived on a neighboring farm, but when he learned that he was to be sold, he escaped to the North. Several years passed, and Tilly yearned for a reunion with her fiancé. When she found out that she was going to be forced to marry another enslaved man, Tilly fled to Baltimore and hid with friends in the city's large Black community. She was able to get word of her whereabouts to her fiancé, who was in Upstate New York, and he contacted Harriet Tubman to arrange for Tilly's rescue.[255]

Toward the end of October 1856, Tubman devised a bold plan that involved traveling in broad daylight by a steamboat and train that would take the two women down the Chesapeake Bay to Baltimore and back across the bay to southern Delaware. Armed with cash provided by Tilly's betrothed, Harriet began her most audacious rescue. According to Thomas Garrett, "She had gone to Philadelphia with the captain of a steamboat, trading though the Delaware and Chesapeake Canal, and had taken the precaution to get from him a certificate of her being a resident of Philadelphia and free."[256] This captain has never been identified, but he may have been known in the Black community as a person who was sympathetic to freedom seekers. Although the record is also unclear about where Tubman met Tilly's fiancé in Upstate New York, it may have been in Frederick Douglass's Rochester home, and if so, he may have sent word to his acquaintances in Baltimore to be on the lookout for Tilly and that "Moses" was on the way to lead her to the promised land.

After Tubman reached Baltimore, the two women went to a steamboat ticket office to buy tickets—not for Philadelphia but for Seaford, Delaware, located in Sussex County. Tubman reasoned that the two Black women would arouse less suspicion traveling south than they would if they were headed north. At that time, most of the steamboat lines in Baltimore docked in the city's basin, today's Inner Harbor. On their way to buy their tickets, Harriet and Tilly passed a group of white men, who began to make rude comments. "Too many likely looking n—rs traveling north these days," one loudly commented. Another asked, "Wonder if these wenches have got a pass?" Tubman and Tilly kept walking. Harriet did not reply to the insults and flaunted the certificate given to her by the steamboat captain as she walked.[257]

There was a line at the ticket office, and the clerk eyed them and said, "You just stand aside, you two; I'll attend to your case by and by." After Tubman and Tilly went to the bow of the steamboat, Harriet began to pray while Tilly trembled. Finally, the clerk approached them and said, "You can come now and get your tickets."[258] A short time later, the steamboat left the basin and traveled past Fell's Point and Fort McHenry on its way down the Patapsco River to the Chesapeake Bay, where it turned south until it reached the Nanticoke River. While on the steamboat, Tubman showed the captain her papers from Philadelphia to Baltimore, and the captain, who was supportive of fugitives, gave them additional travel passes.[259]

After they reached Seaford, Tubman led Tilly to a hotel and booked a room. The next morning, when they were about to leave, a slave trader accosted the two women and attempted to arrest them. Tubman immediately showed him her papers from the steamboat captain. At the same time, the landlord of the hotel intervened, and they were allowed to continue on their way. The railroad to Seaford was not opened until December 1856, about two months after Tilly and Tubman passed through town.[260] Consequently, the two women walked the five miles to Bridgeville. There, they boarded the train to Camden.[261] At Camden, just south of Dover, they met William Brinkley, a free Black operative of the Underground Railroad whom Tubman had met on one of her previous trips through Delaware. Tilly and Tubman took a carriage the remaining fifty miles to Wilmington and Thomas Garrett's office.[262] When she arrived, Tubman announced, "Mr. Garrett, I am here again, out of money and with no shoes to my feet, and God has sent me to you for what I need." Garrett replied, "Harriet, art thou sure thou are not deceived? I cannot find money enough to supply all of God's poor. I had here last week and had to pay eight dollars to clothe and forward them." Tubman was unmoved, "Well, you have got enough for me to pay for a pair of shoes and to pay for my own friend's [Tilly's] passage to Philadelphia. I must have twenty dollars more to enable me to go down to Maryland for a woman and three children." Garrett had recently received a generous amount of money from English abolitionists and was waiting for an opportunity to pass it on to Tubman, who took the money and commented, "Thank you very much. I was sure I could get money from you, but I did not expect so much."[263] After Garrett made arrangements for Tilly to be transported to Philadelphia and from there to Canada to be reunited with her fiancé, Tubman returned to Dorchester County, Maryland, to convince her sister

Rachel to leave Maryland. Rachel's children had been parceled out to other farms, and it proved impossible to get them together for the escape. When Rachel refused to leave, Tubman gathered a small group of other enslaved people and led them to the North.

THE DOVER EIGHT

Agents, sometimes called conductors or pilots, on the Underground Railroad worked in darkness when they met freedom seekers to lead them to the next station. Many of the agents remain anonymous to history, even after slavery was ended by the Civil War, for fear of retribution from their neighbors. In Delaware, many were Quakers. Others were free Black Americans, such as Thomas Otwell, who lived on a farm near Milford. No one recorded the number of fugitives Otwell conducted on his section of the Underground Railroad, but he was a friend of Harriet Tubman. Another conductor, William Brinkley, said that Otwell accompanied Harriet Tubman on some of her visits to Delaware when she stopped at Brinkley's house. Tubman believed that Otwell was a man to be trusted, and she arranged for a group of eight freedom seekers to flee from Maryland through Delaware and Pennsylvania.

Henry Predo was a large, imposing man, and according to William Still of the Pennsylvania Anti-Slavery Society, he was "about twenty-seven years of age, stout and well made, quite black, and no fool." Predo lived in Bucktown, Dorchester County, Maryland, near Harriet Tubman's old home. As happened often, when Predo discovered that his owner intended to sell him to southern slave traders, he planned to escape, but he would not go alone. Five other men and two women joined Predo, and in March 1857, the eight enslaved people left for Delaware.[264] Before the eight freedom seekers left Bucktown, Harriet Tubman advised them about which route to take, and she told them to contact Otwell in Delaware.[265] Unfortunately, the fugitives left on a Sunday, and on Monday morning, they were immediately missed. According to Still, "The excitement over the escape spread very rapidly next morning, and desperate efforts were made to recapture the fugitives, but a few friends there had sympathy and immediately rendered them the needed assistance."[266] The eight fugitives first went to southern Caroline County, where they stopped at the home of Tubman's father, Ben Ross, who "rendered them the needed assistance" before crossing into Delaware.

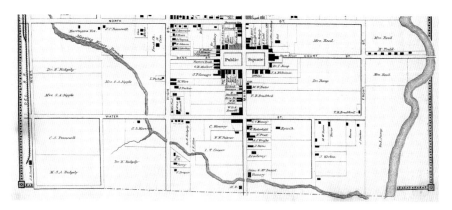

Dover Green, the scene of the escape of the Dover Eight. *Courtesy of the Delaware Public Archives.*

Somewhere south of Dover, the eight fugitives met up with a Delaware Underground Railroad conductor, Otwell, and gave him $8 to lead them north.[267] The conductor was accompanied by a white man, James Hollis, who owned the land that Otwell farmed. The eight fugitives may have been upset with the unexpected appearance of Hollis, a white man. Hollis knew of Otwell's activities on the Underground Railroad, and Otwell assured the fugitives that Hollis was "a great friend of the slaves."[268] While the freedom seekers were on the road, back in Maryland, their owners were organizing a pursuit and began printing posters that offered a $3,000 reward for the capture and return of the fugitives. The reward was massive. At that time, a night in a Wilmington hotel could be had for $1.50, and a round-trip steamboat ticket from Wilmington to Philadelphia cost only $0.60.[269]

By the time the freedom seekers reached Dover, it was four o'clock in the morning. Although it was the capital of Delaware, Dover was a modest town of about three thousand people. The government buildings lined the colonial town green, and when the fugitives arrived, they discovered that a posse from Maryland had reached Dover before them and tacked up reward posters around the town.[270] After Otwell and the freedom seekers met up with Hollis in Dover, they were led to the edge of the town green and into a building, and as they entered, they were directed to go to an upstairs room. As the fugitives filed into the room, one of them spotted bars on the windows and muttered, "I don't like the looks of this."[271]

According to Thomas Garrett, Hollis "had so far succeeded in corrupting his [Otwell's] morals as to induce him to pilot the slaves into

Dover Jail, where they would divide the reward between them."[272] The fugitives attempted to back out of the room when the sheriff, who lived with his family on the lower floor of the building, spotted the Black people attempting to leave. The sheriff had been alerted by Hollis of the freedom seekers' arrival, and he thought that once they entered the room on the second floor, all he needed to do was to shut the door and turn the key. Seeing that plan evaporate, the sheriff retreated to his family's quarters to retrieve his pistol.[273] When Otwell, Hollis and the sheriff blocked the door to the outside, pandemonium broke out, with the sheriff's wife shouting, "Murder!" The fugitives wrestled with the white men to get out of the building.[274] And then, Henry Predo, the leader of the fugitives, picked up a hot andiron and threw burning coals around the room. Amid the choking smoke and burning embers, the two groups struggled with each other until Predo used the andiron to smash open a window, an opportunity the fugitives used to jump to the ground. As Predo left the building, he turned to see the sheriff in his stocking feet aiming a pistol at him. The sheriff pulled the trigger, but it failed to fire.[275]

The fugitives had little idea of which way to go, and they scattered in all directions. Some of them, however, caught up with Otwell. It would have been a simple matter to put a bullet in his brain or slash his throat and leave him bleeding to death. According to Garrett, "Their first impulse was to kill him, but he begged so hard….If they would only spare his life, he would take them to the house of the friend he had promised in the first place to take them to, which he did and then ran off as fast as he could; we have never heard of him since." Garrett commented, "The men were all armed with pistols and knives, and it is a wonder that they acted with so much coolness and discretion. One of the men told me he would have killed him at once had he not thought if he did do it, he would have less chance to escape."[276]

After the commotion died down, Garrett received a report from one of the freedom seekers describing what had happened and asking his advice about how to proceed. Garrett sent a message to a friend in the Dover area, asking him to try to contact the fugitives. Garrett's friend was able to do this, and he led several of the freedom seekers to Garrett's home in Wilmington.[277] During the next couple of days, seven of the group drifted into Garrett's house. According to the *Smyrna Times*, "Thus, they all escaped….Tuesday night, it was currently reported the six were conveyed to the house of a man near Willow Grove, where they were forwarded up the country by the forest roads or rather the Underground Railroad. The other two were seen shortly after the escape from the jail going out of Dover in a northerly direction."[278] The lone person was assumed to have gotten away to Pennsylvania, because Garrett would have heard if he had been captured. Garrett arranged for a small boat to take them across the Christiana River and on to William Still's office in the antislavery society in Philadelphia.[279]

The escape of the freedom seekers, who became known as the "Dover Eight," was widely reported, and slaveholders on Maryland's Eastern Shore were outraged. They were determined to find those responsible for helping the enslaved men run away.[280] Otwell knew that Tubman had helped plan the escape, and he also knew the names of Underground Railroad agents in the Dover-Milford area. He probably knew that the Dover Eight had stopped at Ben Ross's house before they crossed into Delaware. When Tubman learned that they may be

Harriet Beecher Stowe was inspired by the horrors of slavery to write *Uncle Tom's Cabin*. *Courtesy of the Library of Congress.*

implicated in the escape of the Dover Eight, she began to prepare to bring them from Maryland to Pennsylvania. Sarah Bradford, Harriet Tubman's biographer, described the expedition as Tubman's "most venturesome journey."[281] Years later, Garrett wrote, "She brought away her aged parents [both were in their seventies] in a singular manner. They started with an old horse, fitted out in primitive style with a straw collar, a pair of old chaise wheels, with a board on the axle to sit on, another board swung with ropes, fastened to the axle, to rest their feet on. She got her parents…on this rude vehicle to the railroad, put them in the cars….Next day, I furnished her with money to take them all to Canada."[282]

While Rit and Ben Ross were safe, Reverend Samuel Green, a fifty-year-old Black Methodist and a friend of Tubman's, was not so lucky.[283] Green lived in the Bucktown area and was held in high esteem in both the Black and white communities. When it was learned that the Dover Eight had passed by Green's house on their way to Delaware, the authorities searched his house and found several train schedules, a map of Canada and a copy of *Uncle Tom's Cabin*. While some of the materials may have been suspicious, it was against Maryland law to own a copy of Harriet Beecher Stowe's novel, which was considered abolitionist material of "inflammatory character."[284]

Green was arrested, convicted of possession of an abolitionist publication and sentenced to ten years in prison.[285]

Thomas Otwell, the Underground Railroad conductor who betrayed the Dover Eight, was never heard of again. Apparently, he did not divulge what he knew about the clandestine network to conduct freedom seekers through Delaware to Pennsylvania. Having faced a brush with death following the breakout from the Dover Jail, Otwell likely feared retribution if he told the authorities what he knew.

ESCAPE BY SEA

For the four fugitives gathered on Lewes Beach, the broad expanse of Delaware Bay, dotted by sailing vessels, large and small, with the New Jersey shore over the horizon, was an inspiring sight. An occasional steamboat puffed along among the schooners and sloops as the vessels paraded past Cape Henlopen and the town of Lewes. The town faced the sea and was filled with boxy houses with red roofs and white siding inhabited by sturdy pilots who guided ships to Philadelphia and fishermen who plied the waters around Cape Henlopen. The homes on Front Street and Pilottown Road had a clear view of undeveloped Lewes Beach, the bay and the breakwater, and the houses on the east side of town could see the Cape Henlopen Lighthouse standing on an oceanfront sand hill near the Great Dune.

In the 1850s, there were over nine hundred residents in Lewes, and 20 percent of the population were free Black Americans who worked as domestic servants, deckhands, fishermen and shipbuilders in the small shipyards on Lewes Creek.[286] Outside of town, there were over sixty enslaved laborers on nearby farms, and it was on these farms that William Thomas Cope, John Grey, Henry Boice and Isaac White had been held in bondage. Perhaps aided by the town's Black population, the four men slipped past the town's well-kept homes, across Lewes Creek and onto the beach. From there, they would attempt to use a watery track of the Underground Railroad, crossing the bay to the free state of New Jersey.[287]

The four had varying reasons why they wanted to take the dangerous voyage across the Delaware Bay. William Thomas Cope's owner and his wife treated their enslaved laborers harshly and provided them with limited food and clothing. The owner of nineteen-year-old John Grey was David Henry Houston, who once beat and severely slashed an enslaved person for going to church. Houston maintained, "[A slave] and a mule hadn't any feeling."[288]

Henry Boice, the third of the four enslaved men on Lewes Beach, had once been free, but he had been kidnapped into slavery by David Houston, John Grey's owner. The fourth man in the band of fugitives was Isaac White, whose owner was a blacksmith who was given to violent outbursts and often beat him with a wooden plank. After White took two weeks to recover from one of these beatings, he resolved to reach freedom by crossing Delaware Bay. In January 1858, the four men agreed to run away and cross the Delaware Bay to the free state of New Jersey.

A fierce gale was blowing, and the waves were running high on the Delaware Bay as the four young men gathered on the beach. According to William Still, "After much anxious reflection, they finally decided to make their Underground Rail Road exit by water." Living in the Lewes area, the four fugitives were familiar with small boats, and they knew the dangers of being on the bay in a storm. Nonetheless, they secured a skiff (a small flat-bottom boat), and ignoring the growing winds and curling waves of a building storm, the four men cast off. With two of the fugitives at the oars, the men rowed from the beach at Lewes into the stormy bay.

Throughout the night, the men rowed through the rough bay waters toward the New Jersey shore. By the afternoon of the following day, they were in sight of a free state. The traditional signal used by vessels on the water track of the Underground Railroad to indicate that fugitives were on board was to display a yellow light above a blue one, but apparently, the four Lewes Beach runaways did not know this when an oyster boat approached the skiff. The four men decided to take their chances, and they appealed to the captain for assistance. The oyster boat captain was so moved by the plight of the freedom-seeking men that he took them aboard, and they sailed to Philadelphia, where the fugitives stepped ashore as free men.[289]

The four freedom seekers from Lewes Beach were fortunate to meet a friendly waterman, but others who attempted to follow the waterway path of the Delaware Underground Railroad were not so lucky. Thomas Sipple, with his wife, Mary Ann, and Harry Burkett, with his wife, Elizabeth, along with John Purnell and Hale Burton, were enslaved in Worcester County, Maryland. Before they boarded the Underground Railroad, they pooled their money, and the group determined that the safest way to freedom was to cross the Delaware Bay into New Jersey. After traveling on foot into Delaware, they made their way to the bayfront, where they purchased an old batteau, a flat-bottomed boat, for six dollars. None of the four men and two women appeared to have any experience afloat, but after receiving directions to New Jersey (which was not visible from the Delaware beach) and being told the

Freedom seekers used various small craft to escape through the Delaware Bay. *From Still,* Underground Rail Road.

amount of time it would take to cross the Delaware Bay, they started out during the day. Without the North Star or any other aid for navigation, they rowed along the coast of the bay instead of heading in a more northeasterly direction that would have landed them in New Jersey. William Still later wrote, "[T]heir little boat was weak; combined with their lack of knowledge in relation to the imminent danger surrounding them, any intelligent man would have been justified in predicting for them a watery grave long before the bay was half crossed."[290]

Off Kitt's Hummock in Kent County, the freedom seekers were approached by a boat with five white men aboard. When the two boats were next to each other, one of the white men grabbed a chain attached to the boat of the fugitives, and he declared that it was his boat. One of the freedom seekers answered, "This is not your boat; we bought this boat and paid for it." The white men, brandishing guns, threatened to shoot. One of the white men broke an oar over the head of one of the fugitives, knocking him down. Thomas Sipple retaliated by hitting one of the white men, who collapsed into the bottom of his boat. Faced with unexpected resistance, the white men began to row away and started to fire at the fugitives. The white men may have been out hunting for waterfowl, as their weapons were loaded

Unfriendly watermen battled freedom seekers on the Delaware Bay. *From Still,* Underground Rail Road.

with birdshot. The small pellets hit several freedom seekers in their heads and the arms, but none were seriously hurt.

After the white men were driven off, the fugitives took to the oars, changed directions and rowed harder than ever. Eventually, they came to the New Jersey shore. By now, night had fallen, and the fugitives decided to stay with the bateau until daybreak, when they began to scout the area on foot. After walking for a while, they were about a mile from the Cape May Lighthouse when they ran across the captain of an oyster boat. The captain appeared to be friendly, and the freedom seekers asked for directions to Philadelphia. The captain explained how to get to Philadelphia and then offered to take them there for twenty-five dollars. The fugitives agreed, and a short time later, they arrived in the Pennsylvania city, where they went to William Still's office. After a hot bath, fresh clothing and a good meal, the six fugitives boarded the train to Upstate New York to begin their new lives.[291]

The four men who used a skiff to escape from Lewes Beach, the six Maryland freedom seekers in an old batteau and countless other fugitives used the Delaware Bay as their Underground Railroad. Others stowed away on larger vessels to ride the Delaware waters to escape slavery. Aided by Black deckhands, fugitives slipped aboard ships in Norfolk, Richmond and other southern ports that were bound for Wilmington, Delaware, and Philadelphia. Fugitives were often concealed in hiding places deep in the bowels of these ships, and most of these vessels passed Cape Henlopen without stopping on their way to Philadelphia.

In 1854, the steamer *Keystone State* sailed up the Delaware coast on its way from Savannah to Philadelphia. Neither the crew nor the other passengers realized that freedom seeker Edward Davis was aboard. Instead of finding a hiding place in a dark corner of the ship's hold, he hid under a small platform that held a railing that ran along the outside of the ship. During the three days that the *Keystone State* took to reach the Delaware Bay, Davis was constantly pummeled by the waves as he struggled to maintain his precarious position. When the ship rounded Cape Henlopen, Davis was near exhaustion, and he began to call for help. Crewmen from the steamer pulled the fugitive over the rail an onto the deck of the steamer. Captain Robert Hardie of the *Keystone State* believed that Davis was an escaped enslaved laborer, and he docked at New Castle, Delaware, where Hardie sought a court order to take Davis back to Georgia. Davis, however, maintained that he was born in Philadelphia a free man and had been kidnapped into slavery. When the court ruled in favor of Davis, the captain demanded that the penniless fugitive pay for his passage. In one of the few times that Still made light of the plight of runaway enslaved people, he reported, "The only claim the owners of the *Keystone State* or the captain can have on saltwater Davis is for half passenger fare; he came half the way as a fish." Friendly abolitionists, perhaps Thomas Garrett or one of his associates, came down from Wilmington to assist Davis, now nicknamed the "Saltwater Fugitive," when he was set free.[292]

Slaveowners and southern government authorities were well aware that freedom seekers were stowing away on vessels bound for free states. Gangways were watched, and vessels were searched before they were allowed to leave port. In North Carolina, ships were pumped full of smoke in order to drive out any fugitives secreted in hidden places. Abram Galloway and Richard Eden were held in bondage in Wilmington, North Carolina, when the two young men met a captain of a schooner from Wilmington, Delaware, who agreed to assist them by hiding them in his ship. With the captain's help, they believed they could slip aboard the schooner without any difficulty, and they devised a way to survive when the vessel was engulfed in smoke. The two men made long hoods of oilcloth that they slipped over their heads, and they used drawstrings to pull the oilcloths tight around their waists.

Each of the fugitives had a container of water and towels, which they could wet and hold up to their nostrils so they would not breathe in the smoke. Fortunately, when the time came to cast off and leave for Delaware, the schooner, perhaps because it was carrying a cargo of tar and turpentine, was not smoked. After the schooner reached Delaware Bay and sailed on to Philadelphia, the two freedom seekers were welcomed by William Still and the Pennsylvania Anti-Slavery Society. According to Still, "The effects of the turpentine, however…was worse, if possible, than the smoke would have been. The blood was literally drawn from them at every pore in frightful quantities." Still went on to comment that "the invigorating northern air and the kind treatment [of the society] acted like a charm upon them, and they improved very rapidly." The society provided the two men with money for train fare, which sped them on their way to Canada.[293]

Captains Audacious

Edward Davis (who rode halfway to Delaware as a fish), Abram Galloway (who wore an oilcloth hood on his way to freedom) and other unknown fugitives who stole their way aboard ships succeeded mainly by their own wits—with one or two companions and the help of a sympathetic crewman who pointed out hiding places. There were also captains who were fully aware of the fugitives aboard their vessels. Unlike the *Pearl's* Daniel Drayton, who was recruited and founded by white abolitionists, William Still was adamant the antislavery society "never employed agents or captains to go into the South with a view of enticing or running off slaves. So, such when captains operated, they did so with full understanding that they alone were responsible for any failures attending their movements."[294] Captains who made it their business to take ten, twenty or more fugitives at a time on board their ships faced heavy fines, years in jail and, potentially, immediate lynching. Ordinary men avoided these risks, but Captain Alfred Fountain was no ordinary man. Rough and rugged, Fountain was a veteran of numerous sea voyages. The stocky, barrel-chested captain could best any sailor in a forecastle fistfight, but few dared to try. Behind his large eyes and heavy eyebrows was, according to Still, "a man of thought and [who] possessed, in a large measure, those humane traits of character which lead men to sympathize with suffering humanity wherever met with."[295]

Captain Fountain sailed to southern ports to rescue enslaved people from the horrors of slavery, and he did so with the faith of a martyr, but he was not foolish. Still observed, "He was not disposed to be reckless or needlessly to imperil his life or the lives of those he undertook to aid. Nor was he averse to receiving compensation for his service."[296] Fountain frequently called at Wilmington to deliver a cargo of freedom seekers to Thomas Garrett, and in November 1855, he stopped at Norfolk to take on a cargo of wheat and twenty-one fugitives. The disappearance of such a large number of enslaved people aroused speculation that an organized plot had led many of the enslaved to run away. Suspicious fingers pointed at Captain Fountain and his schooner, *Charles T. Ford*.[297] While moored at the Norfolk dock, the audacious captain was loading the last of the wheat aboard his vessel when Ezra T. Summers, the mayor of Norfolk, arrived at the head of a posse armed with long spears and axes. After the posse marched aboard the *Charles T. Ford*, Summers announced that he had come to search Fountain's schooner for runaway enslaved people, to which the captain coolly replied, "Very well. Here I am, and this is my boat; go ahead and search." Summers and his deputies dispersed throughout the schooner, using their spears to poke through the wheat in the vessel's hold. When the members of the posse reported to Summers that the spearing "brought neither blood nor groans," Summers ordered his men, "Take the axes and go to work," and they began to hack away at the deck and other parts of the schooner. Captain Fountain remained unruffled at the posse's haphazard axing that demonstrated "that they were wholly ignorant with regard to boat searching."[298] At this point, Fountain reminded the mayor that he had stood by patiently while his schooner was being chopped up, and the captain said, "Now, if you want to search, give me the axe, and then point out the spot you want opened, and I will open it for you very quick."[299] With that, Fountain took an axe and sent splinters flying from the deck planking, confounding Summers and his posse. Demanding where he should chop next, Fountain struck the deck planking a second time. Confronted by this seeming madman furiously chopping away at his own schooner, Summers and his posse decided that it was time to go. They gave up the search and left the schooner without finding a soul. After Summers left, Fountain raised the sails on the *Charles T. Ford* and set a course for Delaware Bay and Philadelphia, where he delivered his human cargo to the Sill's Anti-Slavery Society.[300] He immediately returned to Virginia to pick up another shipment, which included fourteen freedom seekers. With his passengers securely hidden, Fountain left Norfolk in early 1856 unmolested, but this time, his voyage was interrupted not by slave catchers but by the forces of nature. When Fountain's schooner reached the Delaware River south of Philadelphia, he discovered the winter weather had frozen much of the waterway, and as the ice spread, he was trapped in the frozen river. As they waited for weeks for the river to thaw, the food supply dwindled. Although the schooner was well supplied with salt pork and there were some beans, cornmeal and potatoes on hand, other foodstuffs did not last longer than the first or second week. According to Still, "The sufferings for food, which they were called upon to endure, were beyond description."[301] Thomas Garrett had received word that Fountain's schooner had left Virginia, and the Wilmington stationmaster became concerned when Fountain did not arrive. Garrison sent some of his agents to watch for the arrival of Fountain's overdue schooner. By the third week of March, the ice began thaw, and the *Charles T. Ford* was able to reach the center of Wilmington at the Rocks (the historic landing place of the first Swedish settlers in 1638), where they were met by one of Garrett's associates, who led them to safety.[302]

Within twelve hours of Captain Fountain's arrival, another group of freedom seekers arrived in Wilmington. The second group was on a schooner captained by William Baylis(s) of Wilmington, and they had left Norfolk around the same time Fountain's schooner set sail following his encounter with the mayor. Baylis's schooner had also become ensnared in the ice on the Delaware River. Like Fountain, Baylis was no ordinary man. In 1858, Baylis was described by the *Anti-Slavery Bugle* as "a low, but not thickly set man, quite muscular, about forty-five years of age, and possess[ing] a rather frank, sailor-like appearance than otherwise. Seafaring life has bronzed his complexion and hardened his features to some degree."[303]

A little more than three months after delivering his ice-bound passengers to Wilmington, Baylis was back in Norfolk, loading fifteen freedom seekers of varying ages aboard his schooner. The sailing ship was small enough to fit through the locks of the Chesapeake and Delaware Canal, and as the schooner approached the first set of canal locks, Baylis ordered all the fugitives to go below an enter a small opening in the cabin deck that led to a compartment in the bottom of the schooner. After most of the fugitives entered the damp and cramped space, a large woman had difficulty fitting through the entrance to the hiding place. After much pushing and shoving, she squeezed through the small entrance. After the opening in the deck was covered by an oilcloth carpet, a large table was placed over it.[304] Looking as innocent as Baylis could make it appear, the schooner stopped at the first lock, where it was imprisoned within the wooden walls of the lock as the water level changed. As this was being done, three men came aboard to inspect the schooner. They told Baylis that they had received a telegram from Norfolk alerting them that his schooner was suspected of carrying

Captain Alfred Fountain was an audacious conductor on the waterborne Underground Railroad. *From Still,* Underground Rail Road.

Cape Henlopen, a beacon for freedom seekers. *Courtesy of the Delaware Public Archives.*

fugitives. The three inspectors interrogated Baylis and the mate, and during the discussion, they mentioned that yellow fever was raging in Norfolk. That news made the inspectors more than a little uneasy, but they proceeded to inspect the schooner quickly. When they took up one of the hatches and the foul air billowed out, they claimed it smelled like yellow fever and that no one could live in such a place. Baylis laughed and told them they were welcome to inspect the vessel more thoroughly, but the three men hastily concluded that there were no fugitives on the schooner and left.[305]

The schooner was able to pass through the canal to the Delaware River, where it turned northward. Bypassing Wilmington, Baylis sent a message to Still's Anti-Slavery Society that he would land the passengers at League Island on the edge of Philadelphia at the foot of Broad Street. It was night when the society dispatched three carriages to meet the freedom seekers. At League Island, the schooner moored behind a steep slope that would provide them cover from prying eyes. As the fugitives exited the schooner, they began to slip and slide on the slope back to the river. The members of the antislavery society and the fugitives formed a human chain to help drag the freedom seekers up the incline. The heavy-set woman who had difficulty entering the hiding place on the ship also had difficulty climbing the slope. With several of the fugitives pulling and Captain Baylis pushing, she finally made it up the hill to the waiting carriages, which took the fifteen newly freed people to the society's offices and, from there, sent them to their new homes.[306]

Two years later, in May 1858, Captain Baylis was in Petersburg, Virginia, in command of the small schooner *Keziah*, which was loaded with a cargo of wheat. As he set sail for Delaware Bay, it was reported that several enslaved people from the surrounding area were missing, and it was suspected that they were on the *Keziah*. As Baylis quietly made his way down the James River, a steamer set out in pursuit of his schooner. In a repetition of the *Pearl* incident, the steamer intercepted the *Keziah* before it reached the Chesapeake Bay, and after a search of the schooner, five Black passengers were discovered on board. Baylis was arrested, and the *Keziah* was towed back toward Petersburg. The steamer stopped at City Point to telegraph the authorities in Petersburg that the *Keziah* had been apprehended. The news of the schooner's capture spread quickly through Petersburg, and a large mob assembled on the wharf to get a look at, as the *Petersburg South-Side Democrat* put it, "a real Yankee 'n—r stealer.'"

After the *Keziah* was secured to the dock, Baylis was led ashore, and the *Virginia Index-Appeal* reported, "It was then that the most intense and terrible

Fugitives push and pull their way up the slope at League Island. *From Still,* Underground Rail Road.

excitement ensued, and they had barely reached the shore when a wild shout of indignation went up from the populace, and a desperate effort was made to take possession of them; but for the most vigorous measures and the assistance rendered by several of the calmer citizens, they would have been lynched upon the spot."[307] The authorities were able to get Baylis and his five Black passengers safely through the angry mob to the jail. Baylis was charged with five counts of kidnapping. At his trial, the prosecution maintained that the Black passengers were runaway enslaved laborers who paid between thirty-four and fifty dollars for Baylis to transport them to New Jersey, a free state.

In his defense, Baylis claimed that he did not know that his passengers were enslaved. The captain said that a New Jersey man, whose name in did not know, had agreed to pay for the transport of the five passengers. After deliberating for a half hour, the jury found Baylis guilty of kidnapping on all five counts, and the Wilmington captain was sentenced to eight years in prison for each count, a total of forty years in prison.[308] Baylis was led off to prison, and it is assumed that the five fugitives caught aboard the *Keziah* were taken back into slavery, where they continued to serve their sentence of a lifetime of hard labor.

6

TAKING UP THE TRACKS

They had for more than a century before been regarded as beings of an inferior order, and altogether unfit to associate with the white race, either in social or political relations; and so far inferior, that they had no rights which the white man was bound to respect.
—*Chief Justice Roger B. Taney*[309]

WAR

The Underground Railroad in Delaware reached its peak in the latter part of the 1850s. The older land route in the eastern part of the state had stations at Millsboro, Georgetown, Milford, Frederica and Camden, where it merged with the route on the western side of the state that began at Laurel, ran through Seaford and continued north to Camden to link up with the eastern track. To the north, there were stations in Dover, Smyrna, Blackbird, Odessa, Middletown, Delaware City and New Castle, and there were numerous stations in Wilmington, with the most important one at Thomas Garrett's house.[310] Some freedom seekers from Caroline County, Maryland, traveled from west to east to reach Delaware Bay, where they met friendly Black watermen and others who assisted them in crossing the water to New Jersey. Near Cape Henlopen at the mouth of the bay, Lewes was a common launching point for those making a watery exit from Delaware. At the same time, freedom seekers were traveling surreptitiously aboard ships

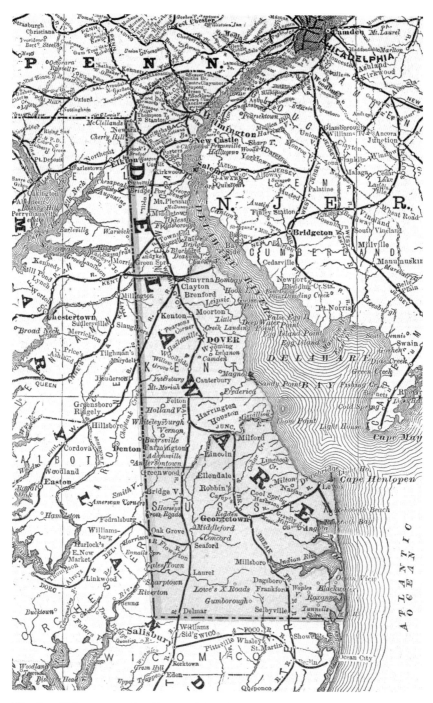

The three Delaware counties. *Courtesy of the Delaware Public Archives.*

from southern ports and around Cape Henlopen through Delaware waters to Pennsylvania and New Jersey.

When the railroad reached Delmar on the Delaware-Maryland border in December 1859, it opened a well-defined path to the North. Although not many freedom seekers slipped aboard the train to Wilmington or Philadelphia, the railroad right-of-way gave fugitives a clear and direct path to the North. The tracks made traveling at night much easier. Using the North Star to establish that they were walking in the right direction, they were able to disregard any roadways or paths that crossed the tracks. If they heard or saw an approaching train, they could easily slip into the underbrush by the side of the tracks until the train passed.

With the structure of the Delaware Underground Railroad more or less settled, Harriet Tubman was spending more time in the North at a home that William Seward, a U.S. senator and fervent abolitionist, enabled her to buy in Auburn, New York, about fifty miles east of Rochester, where Frederick Douglass had a home. By this time, Tubman was well known in abolitionist circles, although publicly, she was not often referred to by name, only as "Moses."

With the Delaware Underground Railroad solidified, the differences between the slave and free states intensified. In 1854, the Kansas-Nebraska Act repealed the Missouri Compromise and stipulated that when these two territories would become states, the residents of those territories would vote on whether to enter the Union as free or slave states. Radicals from both sides flocked to Kansas to be on hand when the territory became a full-fledged state and the vote was taken. This led to a minor civil war that was known as Bloody Kansas. In 1857, the Supreme Court, led by Chief Justice Roger B. Taney, the judge who presided over the trial of Thomas Garrett in 1848, handed down the Dred Scott decision. Scott was an enslaved man who was taken to a free territory, where he sued for his freedom. The court's decision declared that enslaved people were not citizens of the United States and, therefore, could not expect any protection from the federal government. Furthermore, Taney's opinion also stated that Congress had no constitutional authority to ban slavery from the territories.[311] Taney wrote that Black Americans "were, at that time [when the Constitution was written], considered as a subordinate and inferior class of beings, who had been subjugated by the dominant race." The chief justice went on to state, "They had for more than a century before been regarded as beings of an inferior order and altogether unfit to associate with the white race, either in social or political relations; and so

John Brown "of sacred memory."
Courtesy of the Library of Congress.

Frederick Douglass during the Civil
War. *Courtesy of the Library of Congress.*

far inferior, that they had no rights which the white man was bound to respect."[312]

The Dred Scott decision was a complete victory for slaveholders and an infuriating defeat for the abolitionists. Frederick Douglass called it a "vile and shocking abomination."[313] The decision convinced many militant abolitionists that the only way to end slavery was through violence. In the 1850s, Tubman and Douglass became embroiled in John Brown's plot to foment a slave insurrection. Douglass had known of Brown's plan for over a decade, but Douglass thought it impractical, and he was not an enthusiastic supporter of it. Tubman, on the other hand, was more than eager to see the plan put in motion. After a considerable delay, Brown acted without notifying Douglass or Tubman. In October 1859, John Brown raided the federal arsenal at Harper's Ferry, Virginia, in order to distribute weapons to any enslaved people who would fight for their freedom. Brown and his small band of men were eventually overpowered by a detachment of marines led by Colonel Robert E. Lee. Brown was taken to Charleston, Virginia, and tried for treason against the State of Virginia and encouraging a slave insurrection. After a quick trial, he was found guilty and executed.

Many southerners considered Brown a lawless traitor who nearly caused a bloody race war. Many northerners considered him a martyr for the abolitionist cause. For two veterans of the Delaware Underground Railroad, John Brown's raid had potentially deadly repercussions. The Virginia authorities believed correctly that Brown was supported by the abolitionists, and they suspected that Frederick Douglass was one of his accomplices. Douglass was in Philadelphia when he first learned of Brown's raid, and he later wrote, "I saw at once that my old friend had attempted what he had long ago resolved to do."[314] Douglass was well known and easily recognizable from published images of him. He feared that he could be arrested at any time and taken to Virginia, where he would be given a summary trial and executed.[315] In a repeat of his escape from slavery two decades ago, Douglass took a steamer from Philadelphia to New York City, where he was able to take a train to Rochester.[316] From there, Douglass made his way to Canada, where he was safe from arrest. Tubman did not have a public persona like Douglass, and she had much less to fear from staying in the United States.

Nationally, John Brown's raid made slavery the paramount issue of the election of 1860. During a four-way contest, Abraham Lincoln garnered less than 40 percent of the popular vote, but he swept the free states—except for New Jersey—and won a decisive victory in the electoral college.[317] Delaware voted for the proslavery candidate. In December 1860, South Carolina declared, "A geographical line has been drawn across the Union, and all the states north of that line have united in the election of a man to the high office of president of the United States, whose opinions and purposes are hostile to slavery."[318] And with that statement, South Carolina announced its withdrawal from the Union. On April 12, 1861, southerners opened fire on Fort Sumter. The Civil War had begun.

End of the Line

Delaware Underground Railroad

The Delaware Underground Railroad was always an opportunistic organization of sympathetic agents and stationmasters who responded whenever a fugitive appeared on their doorsteps to render whatever immediate need was required. When the Civil War began, and the Union army moved into southern territory, the army became a magnet for fugitives who might have traveled along the Underground Railroad. During the war, the number of freedom seekers passing through the state declined precipitously, and those who once aided the fugitives simply continued their everyday lives. Lacking a formal structure, the Delaware Underground Railroad evaporated, and there was nothing left but to take up other causes.

Virginia families fleeing slavery in 1862. *Courtesy of the Library of Congress.*

Delaware Slaves

When the Civil War began, there were fewer than 1,800 enslaved people in Delaware. In late 1861, President Abraham Lincoln devised a plan to end slavery, stop the war and save thousands of lives. Under Lincoln's plan, the federal government would reimburse Delaware slave owners for their economic loss when they set their enslaved laborers free. All enslaved people over the age of thirty-five would be freed at once; younger enslaved people would be freed in ten years. Congress would establish a fund of $900,000 to compensate slave owners, who would receive a generous payment of around $500 per enslaved laborer. The cost for freeing the enslaved population of Delaware was less than the government spent in a single day fighting the Confederacy. Lincoln believed that the compensated emancipation of Delaware's enslaved population would then spread to other slave states, and it would eliminate the reason for fighting the war. "This," Lincoln said, "was the cheapest and most humane way of ending this war and saving lives."[319]

The plan ignored the political realities in Delaware, whose residents had a deep-rooted aversion to outside meddling in state affairs, and they resented Lincoln's attempt to buy his way out of the Civil War. A resolution was introduced in the Delaware General Assembly that maintained, "When the people of Delaware desire to abolish slavery within her borders, they will do so in their own way."[320] Lincoln's attempt to end the Civil War by compensated emancipation collapsed. When the Emancipation Proclamation went into effect on January 1, 1863, Delaware's enslaved people were not freed. The proclamation applied only to enslaved people in the rebelling states, and Delaware did not join the Confederacy. Delaware's enslaved population had to wait until the ratification of the Thirteenth Amendment in December 1865 to become free. Although the state's enslaved people were free, Delaware did not ratify the Thirteenth Amendment until 1901.

Captain Daniel Drayton and the Passengers on the Pearl

After the *Pearl* was retaken and brought back to Washington, Captain Drayton was tried for his role in the incident, and he was sentenced to twenty years hard labor.[321] The abolitionists, however, did not forget him, and they worked to get the hard-luck captain released. In 1852, after Drayton had spent four years in jail, Senator Charles Sumner of Massachusetts convinced President Franklin Pierce to pardon Drayton, who moved to New England.[322] Drayton was despondent from his inability to find work as a seaman, and on July 7, 1857, the *Wilmington Daily Republican* reported, "Captain Daniel Drayton, who, as the master of the schooner *Pearl* attempted to carry off seventy slaves from Washington, D.C., was captured, sentenced to twenty years' imprisonment, committed suicide at the Mansion House New Bedford, Mass., on Thursday last by taking laudanum."[323]

Most of the freedom seekers on the *Pearl* were condemned to a life of slavery, but Mary and Emily Edmondson caught the attention of New York Methodists, who raised the $2,250 to purchase the sisters' freedom.[324] Harriet Beecher Stowe took an interest in the two young women, and she helped provide for their education.[325] Mary, however, contracted tuberculosis and died in 1853 at the age of twenty. After the Civil War, Emily moved to

Washington, D.C., married and had four children. A friend of Frederick Douglass and Harriet Tubman, Emily Edmondson, a survivor of the ill-fated voyage of the *Pearl*, died on September 15, 1895.[326]

Captain Alfred Fountain

After the Civil War began, the bold captain of the *Charles T. Ford* had his schooner burned when the Confederates abandoned Norfolk, Virginia. With his ship gone, Fountain decided to enlist in the Union army and then dropped out of the historical record.[327]

Captain William Baylis

In 1858, the captain of the *Keziah* was sentenced to forty years in prison, but when Richmond was overrun by the Union forces in 1865, he was released. Baylis returned to Wilmington, and on February 10, 1881, the *Delaware State Journal* ran this simple death notice: "In this city [Wilmington, Delaware] on 7th inst., William B. Baylis, in the 70th year of his age, [died]."[328]

Peter Steel

After Peter Steel (Friedman) united with his brother, William, he was determined to rescue his wife and children from slavery. Peter hired Seth Conklin, an experienced conductor on the Underground Railroad, to help free Peter's family. The expedition ended in disaster. Conklin was murdered, and Peter's family remained enslaved. Peter was able to contact his family's owner, who agreed to sell Peter's wife and children for $3,000. Undaunted by the enormous sum, Peter began a speaking tour to raise the necessary money. Two years later, he had the money. One of Peter's sons had a two-year-old boy, and when the money was presented to the owner, he demanded an extra $300 for the child. Peter did not have the $300, and the boy was left behind when the rest of the family journeyed to New Jersey, where they lived near Peter's siblings. Fortunately, after the end of the Civil War and the abolition of slavery, Peter's grandson was able to be reunited with the rest of the family. Peter Steel lived to see his grandson two years before he died of pneumonia in 1867.[329]

William Still

By the time the Civil War ended, along with the Underground Railroad, William Still had interrogated nearly one thousand freedom seekers who passed through the Pennsylvania Anti-Slavery Society's offices. In 1872, William collected the notes of his interviews, letters and profiles of members of the Underground Railroad and published them as the *Underground Railroad Records.* The book went through several editions, and it remains an invaluable source of information about the men and women who fled slavery. After the Civil War, Still was associated with several reform movements, but he soon found himself out of step with the younger reformers. On July 15, 1902, the *Washington Evening Times* announced Still's death, stating that, among other things, "He was secretary of the Pennsylvania Abolition Society, president for twenty-five years of the board of managers of the Home for Aged and Infirm Colored People, a member of the board of managers of the Home for Colored Children, and president of the Berean Building and Loan Association."[330] The *Wilmington Evening Journal* stated that this son of parents who were once were enslaved "leaves a fortune estimated at between $750,000 and $1,000,000."[331] In recognition of his Underground Railroad work, the Caroline County Historical Society maintains the William Still Family Interpretive Center and Historic Site in Denton, Maryland.

Frederick Douglass

Frederick Douglass in the 1880s. *Courtesy of the Library of Congress.*

During the Civil War, Frederick Douglass prodded President Lincoln to issue an order freeing the enslaved and to recruit Black troops. After the war, he served in a number of government posts, and he continued to advocate for social causes, particularly women's right to vote. His wife, Anna Murray Douglass, who assisted Douglass in his flight for freedom, died in 1882.[332] Two years later, Douglass married Helen Pitts, a longtime friend and an advocate for women's rights and other causes. Born in 1838, the year Douglass escaped from slavery through Delaware, she was two decades younger than Douglass. She was also white. At that time, it was not uncommon for widowers to marry younger brides. It was, however, unusual for a Black man to marry a white woman, and that sparked a bit of controversy among some family members and the public. Frederick and Helen remained happily married until 1895, when Douglass died of an apparent heart attack in his Washington, D.C. home. His death was widely reported, and many newspapers printed a summary of his life.[333]

In recent years, statues have been erected of Frederick Douglass in Baltimore; Washington, D.C.; and a number of other locations, including one in front of the Talbot County Courthouse in Easton, near the place where he was held after his first attempt to escape from slavery.

Harriet Tubman

After the firing on Fort Sumter, Harriet Tubman continued to act as the Moses of her people. Attached to the Union army in coastal South Carolina, whose marshes and wetlands resembled her home on the Eastern Shore of Maryland, Tubman served as a nurse, spy and scout. As the northern forces

Formerly enslaved people freed by Union forces in South Carolina. *Courtesy of the Library of Congress.*

advanced, she led hundreds of enslaved people behind the Union lines. After the war, like Douglass, Tubman was active in the women's rights movement. Unlike Douglass, her death in 1913 attracted little notice in the newspapers.

On October 3, 2012, a large statue titled *Unwavering Courage in the Pursuit of Freedom* was dedicated in downtown Wilmington. The statue depicts Harriet Tubman as she appeared on the Underground Railroad, with Thomas Garrett pointing the way. In March 2017, the Maryland Park Service, in partnership with the National Park Service, opened the Harriet Tubman Underground Railroad State Park and Visitor Center near Tubman's childhood

Harriet Tubman in the early twentieth century. *Courtesy of the Library of Congress.*

home south of Cambridge, Maryland. The park serves as the trailhead for the 125-mile-long Harriet Tubman Underground Railroad Byway, which leads to Tubman and Underground Railroad heritage sites, including the Harriet Tubman Museum and Educational Center in Cambridge, Maryland.

Thomas Garrett

After the Delaware Underground Railroad ended during the Civil War, Thomas Garrett devoted his time to a hardware business. When the Fifteenth Amendment guaranteed Black men the right to vote in 1870, a large celebration was held in Wilmington, with Garrett riding in an open carriage pulled through the streets, surrounded by his Black and white friends and banners that read, "Our Moses."[334]

A year later, Frederick Douglass's newspaper, the *New National Era*, announced on February 2, 1871, "Thomas Garrett, who died full of years and honor, on the morning of January 25, at the ripe age of eighty-one, was a man of no common character. He was an abolitionist from his youth up, and…it had no more faithful worker in its ranks than Thomas Garrett."[335] His funeral was held at the Friends Meeting House in Wilmington, and the *New National Era* said, "[It] was conducted with the plainness of form which

Children assisted by Thomas Garrett. *From Still*, Underground Rail Road.

characterizes the society of which he was a member. There was no display, no organization, nothing whatever to distinguish this from ordinary funerals, except the outpouring of people of every creed, condition and color, to follow the remains to their last resting place."[336] For over an hour, a solemn procession of mourners passed by the open coffin to pay their respects. This was followed by remarks from several people who knew Garrett well, including Lucretia Mott, the noted abolitionist and advocate for women's rights. Shortly after three o'clock, the coffin was closed and carried on the shoulders of four Black men from the meetinghouse to the burial grounds and Thomas Garrett's final resting place.[337] The unquestioned hero of the Delaware Underground Railroad who assisted 2,700 fugitives to freedom, Garrett lies beneath a simple stone marker.

NOTES

Prologue

1. Douglass, *Narrative*, 97.
2. Still, *Underground Rail Road*, iv–vi; 63.
3. Douglass *Narrative*, 9.
4. Ibid., 11.
5. Ibid., 13–14; Blight, *Douglass*, 24.
6. Douglass, *Narrative*, 14.
7. Douglass, *My Bondage*, 103.
8. Douglass, *Narrative*, 13.
9. Ibid.
10. Larson, *Bound for the Promised Land*, 40.
11. Bradford, *Scenes in the Life*, 74–75.
12. Ibid., 13.
13. Larson, *Bound for the Promised Land*, 42–43.
14. Bradford, *Scenes in the Life*, 65.
15. Larson, *Bound for the Promised Land*, 62–63.

Chapter 1

16. "Dorchester County," *Maryland Gazette*.
17. Smith, *Generall Historie*, 117–18.

18. Woolley, *Savage Kingdom*, 353–54, 363.
19. Munroe, *Colonial Delaware*, 4–7.
20. Ibid., 61.
21. Horle, *Records*, 1,194.
22. Heinegg, *Free African Americans*, 707; "Transform Delmarva History?" *Daily Times*.
23. "Run Away…," *Maryland Gazette*.
24. "Dorchester County," *Maryland Gazette*.
25. Advertisements, *Maryland Gazette*.
26. Williams, *Slavery and Freedom*, 75–76.
27. Ibid., 15–16.
28. Falconbridge, *Account of the Slave Trade*, 19–21.
29. Williams, *Slavery and Freedom*, 15–16.
30. Ibid., 15–16, 51–52; Horle, *Records*, 170.

Chapter 2

31. Bayley, *Some Remarkable Incidents*, 8.
32. Jefferson's Monticello, "Life of Sally Hemings."
33. Pennsylvania Abolition Society, "William Still."
34. Kashatus, *William Still*, 33–34.
35. New Jersey Historical Commission, "New Jersey."
36. Williams, *Slavery and Freedom*, 148, 159.
37. U.S. Const., art. IV, § 3.
38. U.S. Const., art. I, § 9.
39. "Philadelphia," *National Gazette*.
40. "One Hundred Fifty Dollars Reward," *Delaware Gazette*; "50 Dollars Reward," *Delaware Gazette*.
41. Hancock, "William Morgan's Autobiography," 48.
42. Ibid., 49.
43. U.S.History.org, "Fugitive Slave Law."
44. Bayley, *Some Remarkable Incidents*, 38.
45. Ibid., 39.
46. Ibid., 2–7.
47. Ibid., 8.
48. Ibid., 18.
49. Tunnell, "Manufacture of Iron," 85–91.
50. Swank, *Manufacture of Iron*, 237–39.

51. Johnstone, *Address*, 32.

52. Ibid., 33–34.

53. Ibid., 41.

54. Williams, *Slavery and Freedom*, 79.

55. DePuydt, "Free at Last," 175–76.

56. Williams, *Slavery and Freedom*, 141.

57. Ibid.

58. Still, *Underground Rail Road*, 37–38.

59. Ibid.

60. McGowan, *Station Master*, 27.

61. Still, *Underground Rail Road*, 624.

62. Ibid., 625.

63. McGowan, *Station Master*, 37.

64. Roth, *Monster's Handsome Face*, 10–11, 14–15.

65. Torrey, *Portraiture*, 47.

66. "Kidnapping," *African Observer*, 41.

67. Ibid., 39–43.

68. Northup, *Twelve Years*, 57, 303.

69. *American Watchman and Delaware Advertiser*, July 7, 1826.

70. "Kidnapping," *African Observer*, 45.

71. Ibid.

72. "Horrible Development," *Niles Register*.

73. "Murders," *Niles Register*.

74. "Patty Cannon," *Delaware Register*.

75. Ibid.

76. Harsmanden, *New York Conspiracy*, viii.

77. Williams, *Slavery and Freedom*, 74.

78. Ibid.

79. Ibid., 74–75.

80. Ibid., 194.

Chapter 3

81. Douglass, *Narrative*, 78.

82. Bordewich, *Canaan*, 115, 271.

83. Douglass, *Life and Times*, 198–99.

84. Williams, *Slavery and Freedom*, 204–6.

85. Ibid., 51–52, 204–6.

86. Vincent, *History*, 17.
87. Franklin and Schweninger, *Runaway*, 86.
88. "Notice," *Wilmingtonian and Delaware Advertiser*.
89. "Meeting," *Wilmingtonian and Delaware Advertiser*; Jordan, *Slavery*, 37.
90. Douglass, *Narrative*, 90–91.
91. McGowan, *Station Master*, 87–88.
92. Ibid.
93. "$200 Reward," *Delaware Gazette and American Watchman*.
94. "$50 Reward," *Delaware Gazette and American Watchman*.
95. Bordewich, *Canaan*, 5.
96. Still, *Underground Rail Road*, v–vii.
97. Ibid., vii–viii.
98. Ibid., xviii.
99. Crew, "Saga," 68.
100. Ibid., 65.
101. Still, *Underground Rail Road*, xxxii–xxxiii.
102. Ibid.
103. Crew, "Saga," 68.
104. Douglass, *Narrative*, 16–17.
105. Ibid., 20.
106. Ibid., 30.
107. Ibid.
108. Ibid., 32–33.
109. Ibid., 37.
110. Ibid., 33.
111. Ibid., 34–36.
112. Ibid., 35.
113. Ibid., 45–46.
114. Ibid., 79.
115. Ibid.
116. Ibid., 77.
117. Ibid.
118. Ibid., 80–82.
119. Ibid., 82–84.
120. Ibid., 85.
121. Ibid., 86.
122. Ibid., 87.
123. Ibid., 88.
124. Douglass, *My Bondage*, 31; "Preservationists…," *Baltimore Sun*.

125. Douglass, *Life and Times*, 246.
126. Ibid., 246–47.
127. Blight, *Douglass*, 81.
128. Douglass, *Life and Times*, 247–48.
129. Ibid.
130. Ibid.
131. Ibid., 249.
132. Ibid.
133. Douglass, *Life and Times*, 255.
134. Blight, *Douglass*, 87–88.
135. McGowan, *Station Master*, 52.
136. Ibid., 55–57.
137. Still, *Underground Rail Road*, 746–47.
138. "Slaveholding Law…," *Pennsylvania Freeman*.
139. Ibid.
140. "Garrett and Hunn," *Pennsylvania Freeman*.
141. McGowan, *Station Master*, 209.
142. Ibid., 164–65.

Chapter 4

143. McGowan, *Station Master*, 171.
144. Ricks, *Escape*, 23.
145. Drayton, *Personal Memoir*, 10.
146. Ibid., 10–11.
147. Ibid., 16.
148. Ibid.
149. Ricks, *Escape*, 21.
150. Ibid., 22.
151. Ibid.
152. Drayton, *Personal Memoir*, 23.
153. Ibid., 25.
154. Ricks, *Escape*, 28; Drayton, *Personal Memoir*, 70.
155. Drayton, *Personal Memoir*, 29.
156. Ricks, *Escape*, 7–9.
157. Ibid., 8.
158. Drayton, *Personal Memoir*, 30.
159. Ibid.

160. Ibid.
161. Ricks, *Escape*, 54.
162. Ibid., 55.
163. Drayton, *Personal Memoir*, 31.
164. Ibid., 33.
165. Ricks, *Escape*, 75.
166. Ibid., 77–78.
167. Ibid., 78.
168. Painter, "Fugitives of the *Pearl*," 248.
169. Ricks, *Escape*, 84.
170. Painter, "Fugitives of the *Pearl*," 250.
171. Larson, *Bound for the Promised Land*, 62.
172. Ibid., 64.
173. Ibid., 65.
174. Ibid., 72–73.
175. Bradford, *Moses*, 26.
176. Larson, *Bound for the Promised Land*, 64.
177. Ibid., 78.
178. Bradford, *Moses*, 28.
179. Ibid., 29.
180. Larson, *Bound for the Promised Land*, 81.
181. Ibid., 83.
182. Gray, *National Waterway*, 52.
183. Bradford, *Moses*, 30.
184. Ibid., 32.
185. McGowan, *Station Master*, 209.
186. Ibid.
187. Ibid., 210.
188. U.S. Const., art. I, § 2.
189. McGowan, *Station Master*, 210.
190. Ibid.
191. Ibid.
192. Ibid.
193. Stowe, *Uncle Tom*, 116; Stowe, *A Key*, 123.
194. Larson, *Bound for the Promised Land*, 85.
195. Ibid., 89.
196. Gray, *National Waterway*, 66.
197. Ibid., 106.
198. Larson, *Bound for the Promised Land*, 90.

199. Brewington, *Chesapeake Bay*, 5.
200. Larson, *Bound for the Promised Land*, 90.
201. Ibid.
202. Ibid.
203. Bradford, *Moses*, 112.
204. Clinton, *Harriet Tubman*, 84; Bradford, *Scenes in the Life*, 77.
205. Bradford, *Scenes in the Life*, 24–25.
206. Larson, *Bound for the Promised Land*, 92.
207. Douglass, *Life and Times*, 328–29.
208. Ibid., 329.
209. Bradford, *Scenes in the Life*, 6–7.
210. Ibid., 7.
211. Ibid.
212. Larson, *Bound for the Promised Land*, 86.

Chapter 5

213. Douglass, *My Bondage*, 127–28.
214. Still, *Underground Railroad*, 566.
215. Ibid., 569.
216. Ibid., 572.
217. Ibid., 575.
218. Ibid.
219. Ibid., 57.
220. Douglass, "Speech."
221. Slaughter, *Bloody Dawn*, 11.
222. Ibid., 47; Kashatus, *William Still*, 71.
223. Slaughter, *Bloody Dawn*, 52; Kashatus, *William Still*, 72; Still, *Underground Rail Road*, 350.
224. Slaughter, *Bloody Dawn*, 52–53; Kashatus, *William Still*, 72; Still, *Underground Rail Road*, 349.
225. Slaughter, *Bloody Dawn*, 58.
226. Ibid., 60; Kashatus, *William Still*, 72.
227. Slaughter, *Bloody Dawn*, 61.
228. Ibid., 62; Kashatus, *William Still*, 73.
229. Slaughter, *Bloody Dawn*, 64; Kashatus, *William Still*, 74; Still, *Underground Rail Road*, 350.
230. Kashatus, *William Still*, 74.

231. Ibid.; Slaughter, *Bloody Dawn*, 69.

232. Kashatus, *William Still*, 74; Slaughter, *Bloody Dawn*, 69.

233. Slaughter, *Bloody Dawn*, 69.

234. Kashatus, *William Still*, 75.

235. Ibid.

236. Ibid.

237. Slaughter, *Bloody Dawn*, 115.

238. Ibid., 123.

239. Douglass, "Speech."

240. Bradford, *Scenes in the Life*, 57.

241. Larson, *Bound for the Promised Land*, 110–11.

242. Still, *Underground Rail Road*, 297–98.

243. Ibid.

244. Ibid., 296.

245. Bradford, *Scenes in the Life*, 58.

246. Larson, *Bound for the Promised Land*, 96.

247. Harriet Tubman Museum of New Jersey, "Harriet Tubman."

248. Bradford, *Scenes in the Life*, 58.

249. Bradford, *Scenes in the Life*, 59; Larson, *Bound for the Promised Land*, 111.

250. Larson, *Bound for the Promised Land*, 113–14.

251. Blockson, *Underground Railroad*, 146.

252. Still, *Underground Rail Road*, 296.

253. Larson, *Bound for the Promised Land*, 117.

254. Ibid.

255. McGowan, *Station Master*, 171–72.

256. Ibid.

257. Bradford, *Moses*, 59.

258. Ibid.

259. McGowan, *Station Master*, 172.

260. Hayman, *Rails*, 23.

261. McGowan, *Station Master*, 171–72.

262. Larson, *Bound for the Promised Land*, 321.

263. McGowan, *Station Master*, 171.

264. Still, *Underground Railroad*, 72–73.

265. Larson, *Bound for the Promised Land*, 138.

266. Still, *Underground Rail Road*, 73.

267. Larson, *Bound for the Promised Land*, 138.

268. McGowan, *Station Master*, 108, 179.

269. "Indian Queen Hotel," *Commonwealth*; "Trips Resumed," *Daily Enterprise*.

270. McGowan, *Station Master*, 181.
271. Ibid., 179.
272. Ibid.
273. Ibid., 180.
274. "Runaway Slaves," *Smyrna Times*.
275. Still, *Underground Rail Road*, 73.
276. McGowan, *Station Master*, 180.
277. Ibid.
278. "Runaway Slaves," *Smyrna Times*.
279. Larson, *Bound for the Promised Land*, 140; McGowan, *Station Master*, 180.
280. Larson, *Bound for the Promised Land*, 141.
281. Bradford, *Scenes in the Life*, 80.
282. McGowan, *Station Master*, 192–93.
283. Larson, *Bound for the Promised Land*, 140.
284. Ibid., 142.
285. Ibid.
286. Kotowski and Rogers, "Boat Building."
287. Still, *Underground Rail Road*, 481–83.
288. Ibid., 495–96.
289. Ibid., 481–83.
290. Ibid., 530.
291. Ibid., 528–30.
292. Ibid., 243–45.
293. Ibid., 150–52.
294. Ibid., 166.
295. Ibid.
296. Ibid.
297. Larson, *Bound for the Promised Land*, 153.
298. Still, *Underground Rail Road*, 167.
299. Ibid.
300. Ibid., 167–68.
301. Ibid., 334.
302. Ibid., 325.
303. "Pursuit and Recovery," *Antislavery Bugle*.
304. Still, *Underground Rail Road*, 561.
305. Ibid., 561–62.
306. Ibid., 559–60.
307. "Slavery Reminiscence," *Wilmington Daily Republican*.
308. Ibid.

Chapter 6

309. National Archives, "*Dred Scott.*"
310. Blockson, *Underground Railroad*, 146.
311. National Archives, "*Dred Scott.*"
312. Ibid.
313. Douglass, "Speech."
314. Douglass, *Life and Times*, 376.
315. Ibid., 377.
316. Ibid.
317. Hancock, *Delaware*, 35.
318. Avalon Project, "Declaration of the Immediate Causes."
319. Hancock, *Delaware*, 107.
320. Williams, *Slavery and Freedom*, 175.
321. Pacheco, *The* Pearl, 159.
322. Ibid., 230.
323. Ibid., 238; "Suicide," *Daily Republican*.
324. Pacheco, *The* Pearl, 129–30.
325. Ibid., 135–37.
326. "Anacostia," *Evening Star*.
327. McGowan, *Station Master*, 152; Foner, *Gateway*, 25.
328. "Deaths," *Delaware State Journal*.
329. Crew, "Saga," 68.
330. "Noted Colored Abolitionist," *Evening Times*.
331. "Still Is Dead," *Evening Journal*.
332. Blight, *Douglass*, 629.
333. "Douglass," *Middletown Transcript*.
334. "Thomas Garrett," *New National Era*.
335. Ibid.
336. "Late Thomas Garrett," *New National Era*.
337. Ibid.; McGowan, *Station Master*, 129–30.

BIBLIOGRAPHY

Ball, Charles. *A Narrative of the Life and Adventures of Charles Ball*. Pittsburgh: John T. Shyrock, 1854.

Bayley, Solomon. *Narrative of Some Remarkable Incidents in the Life of Solomon Bayley*. London: Harvey and Darton, 1825.

Blight, David W. *Frederick Douglass, Prophet of Freedom*. New York: Simon and Schuster Paperbacks, 2018.

Blockson, Charles. *The Underground Railroad*. New York: Berkley Books, 1994.

Bordewich, Fergus. *Bound for Canaan*. New York: HarperCollins, 2005.

Bradford, Sarah H. *The Moses of Her People*. New York: Geo. R. Lockwood and Son, 1897.

———. *Scenes in the Life of Harriet Tubman*. Auburn, NY: W.J. Moses, Printer, 1869.

Brewington, M.V. *Chesapeake Bay Sailing Craft*. St. Michaels, MD: Chesapeake Bay Maritime Museum, 1966.

Clinton, Catherine. *Harriet Tubman, The Road to Freedom*. New York: Back Bay Books, Little, Brown and Company, 2004.

Crew, Spencer R. "The Saga of Peter Still." 24th Annual Louis Faugères Bishop Lecture. Rutgers University, New Brunswick, NJ. February 23, 2009.

DePuydt, Peter J. "Free at Last, Someday: Senator Outerbridge Horsey And Manumission in the Nineteenth Century." *Pennsylvania History: A Journal of Mid-Atlantic Studies* 76, no. 2 (spring 2009): 164–77.

Douglass, Frederick. *Life and Times of Frederick Douglass*. Hartford: Park Publishing, 1882.

———. *My Bondage and Freedom*. New York: Miller, Orton and Mulligan, 1855.

———. *Narrative of the Life of Fredrick Douglass, An American Slave*. London: H.G. Collins, 1881. Drayton, Daniel. *Personal Memoir of Daniel Drayton*. Boston: Bela Marsh and American and Foreign Anti-Slavery Society, 1855.

Falconbridge, Alexander. *An Account of the Slave Trade on the Coast of Africa*. London: J. Phillips and George Yard, 1788.

Foner, Eric. *Gateway to Freedom*. New York: W.W. Norton, 2015.

Franklin, John Hope, and Loren Schweninger. *Runaway Slaves*. New York: Oxford University Press, 1999.

Gray, Ralph D. *The National Waterway*. Urbana: University of Illinois Press, 1967.

Hancock, Harold B. *Delaware During the Civil War*. Wilmington: Delaware Heritage Commission, 2003.

———. "William Morgan's Autobiography and Diary: Life in Sussex County, 1780–1857." *Delaware History* 19, no. 1 (spring–summer 1980): 39–52.

Harsmanden, Daniel. *The New York Conspiracy*. Boston: Beacon Press, 1971.

Hayman, John C. *Rails Along the Chesapeake*. N.p.: Marvadel Publishers, 1979.

Heinegg, Paul. *Free African Americans of North Carolina, Virginia, and South Carolina From the Colonial Period to About 1820*. Vol. 2. Baltimore: Genealogical Publishing Company, 2005.

Horle, Craig, ed. *Records of the Courts of Sussex County Delaware, 1677–1710*. Vol. 2. Philadelphia: University of Pennsylvania Press, 1991.

Johnstone, Abraham. *The Address of Abraham Johnstone, A Black Man*. Philadelphia: printed for the purchasers, 1797.

Jordan, Ryan P. *Slavery and the Meetinghouse, The Quakers and the Abolitionist Dilemma, 1820–1865*. Bloomington: Indiana University Press, 2007.

Kashatus, William C. *William Still, the Underground Railroad and the Angel at Philadelphia*. South Bend, IN: University of Notre Dame Press, 2021.

Kotowski, Bob, and Steve Rogers. "Boat Building Lewes: Then and Now." *Journal of the Lewes Historical Society* 15 (November 2012): 47–51.

Larson, Kate Clifford. *Bound for the Promised Land, Harriet Tubman, Portrait of an American Hero*. New York: One World Random House, 2003.

McGowan, James. *Station Master on the Underground Railroad*. Jefferson, NC: McFarland and Company, 2005.

Mitchell, Reverend W.M. *The Underground Railroad from Slavery to Freedom*. London: William Tweedie, 1860.

Munroe, John A. *Colonial Delaware*. Wilmington: Delaware Heritage Press, 2003.

Northup, Solomon. *Twelve Years a Slave*. Auburn, NY: Miller, Orton and Mulligan, 1854.

Pacheco, Josephine. *The* Pearl. Chapel Hill: University of North Carolina Press, 2005.

Painter, John H. "The Fugitives of the *Pearl*." *Journal of Negro History* 1, no. 3 (June 1916): 243–54.

Rickard, Kate E.R. *The Kidnapped and the Ransomed*. New York: Miller, Orton and Mulligan, 1856.

Ricks, Mary Kay. *Escape on the* Pearl. New York: Harper Perennial, 2007.

Roth, Hal. *The Monster's Handsome Face*. Vienna, MD: Nanticoke Books, 1998.

Siebert, Wilbur H. *The Underground Railroad from Slavery to Freedom*. New York: Macmillan Company, 1899.

Slaughter, Thomas P. *Bloody Dawn*. New York: Oxford University Press, 1991.

Smedley, R.C. *History of the Underground Railroad*. Lancaster, PA: John A. Hiestand, 1883.

Smith, John. *The Generall Historie of Virginia, New England and the Summer Isles*. Glasgow, UK: John MacLehose and Sons, 1907.

Still, William. *Underground Rail Road Records*. Philadelphia: William Still, Publisher, 1886.

Stowe, Harriet Beecher. *A Key to Uncle Tom's Cabin*. London: Sampson Low, Son and Company, 1853.

———. *Uncle Tom's Cabin*. London: John Casseli, 1852.

Swank, James. *The Manufacture of Iron in All Ages*. Philadelphia: American Iron and Steel Association, 1892.

Switala, William J. *Underground Railroad in Delaware, Maryland, and West Virginia*. Mechanicsburg, PA: Stackpole Books, 2004.

Torrey, Jesse. *A Portraiture of Domestic Slavery in the United States*. Philadelphia: John Bioren, Printer, 1817.

Tunnell, James M., Jr. "The Manufacture of Iron in Sussex County." *Delaware History* 4, no. 2 (September 1954): 85–91.

Vincent, Francis. *A History of the State of Delaware*. Philadelphia: John Campbell, 1870.

Williams, William H. *Slavery and Freedom in Delaware, 1639–1865*. Wilmington, DE: Scholarly Resources Inc., 1996.

Woolley, Benjamin. *Savage Kingdom: The True Story of Jamestown, 1607, and the Settlement of America*. New York: Harper Collins, 2007.

Online Sources

Avalon Project. "Declaration of the Immediate Causes Which Induce and Justify the Secession of South Carolina from the Federal Union." Documents in Law, History and Diplomacy. http://avalon.law.yale.edu/19th_century/csa_scarsec.asp.

Douglass, Frederick. "Speech on the Dred Scott Decision, May 1857." University of Tennessee–Chattanooga. https://www.utc.edu/sites/default/files/2021-01/fddredscottspeechexcerpt2018.pdf.

Frederick Douglass Project Writings: The Fugitive Slave Law. "Speech to the National Free Soil Convention at Pittsburgh, August 11, 1852." https://rbscp.lib.rochester.edu/4385.

Harriet Tubman Museum of New Jersey. "Harriet Tubman Museum." https://www.harriettubmanmuseum.org/about.

Independence Hall in American Memory. "Tamor/Euphemia Williams (Mahala Purnell)." http://www.independencehall-americanmemory.com/slavery-and-freedom/fugitive-slave-hearings-of-the-1850s/euphemia-williams/.

Jefferson's Monticello. "The Life of Sally Hemings." https://www.monticello.org/sallyhemings/.

National Archives. "The Constitution of the United States: A Transcription." America's Founding Documents. https://www.archives.gov/founding-docs/constitution-transcript.

———. "Dred Scott v. Stanford." https://www.archives.gov/milestone-documents/dred-scott-v-sandford.

New Jersey Historical Commission. "New Jersey: The Last Northern State to End Slavery." https://nj.gov/state/historical/his-2021-juneteenth.shtml.

Pennsylvania Abolition Society. "William Still: An African American Abolitionist." http://stillfamily.library.temple.edu/stillfamily/exhibits/show/william-still/people-and-places/pennsylvania-abolition-society.

U.S. History.org. "Fugitive Slave Act of 1793". President's House in Philadelphia. https://www.ushistory.org/presidentshouse/history/slaveact1793.php.

Newspapers

American Watchman and Delaware Advertiser. July 7, 1826.

Antislavery Bugle. "Pursuit and Recovery of Fugitive Slaves." June 19, 1858.

Baltimore Sun. "Preservationists…." September 23, 2021.

Commonwealth. "Almond's Indian Queen Hotel." August 14, 1858.

Daily Enterprise. "Trips Resumed." April 23, 1858.

Daily Republican. "Suicide of Capt. Drayton." July 2, 1857.

Daily Times. "A Find to Transform Delmarva History?" December 7, 2017.

Delaware Gazette. "50 Dollars Reward." October 11, 1809.

———. "One Hundred Fifty Dollars Reward." October 11, 1809.

Delaware Gazette and American Watchman. "$50 Reward." June 4, 1930.

———. "$200 Reward." June 4, 1830.

Delaware Register. "$50 Reward." June 4, 1830.

———. "Patty Cannon." May 23, 1829.

Delaware State Journal. "Deaths." February 10, 1881.

Evening Journal. "William Still Is Dead." July 15, 1902.

Evening Star. "Anacostia." September 17, 1895.

Evening Times. "Death of a Noted Colored Abolitionist." July 15, 1902.

"Kidnapping." *African Observer* 1, no. 1 (May 1827): 37–47.

Maryland Gazette. Advertisements. August 23, 1745.

———. "Dorchester County." April 15, 1746.

———. "Run Away…." May 6, 1729.

Middletown Transcript. "Frederick Douglass." February 23, 1895.

National Gazette. "Philadelphia." July 11, 1792.

New National Era. "The Late Thomas Garrett." February 2, 1871.

———. "Thomas Garrett." February 2, 1871.

Niles Register. "A Horrible Development." April 25, 1829.

———. "Murders in Delaware." May 23, 1829.

Pennsylvania Freeman. "More Slaveholding Law…." June 1, 1848.

———. "Thomas Garrett and John Hunn." June 8, 1848.

Smyrna Times. "Runaway Slaves." March 18, 1857.

Wilmington Daily Republican. "A Slavery Reminiscence." February 23, 1887.

Wilmingtonian and Delaware Advertiser. "Meeting." December 26, 1826.

———. "Notice." August 17, 1826.

INDEX

Place names are in Delaware unless otherwise noted.

Z

ABOUT THE AUTHOR

Photograph by Tom Morgan.

Michael Morgan has been writing freelance newspaper articles on the history of coastal Delaware for over three decades. He is the author of the "Delaware Diary," which appears weekly in the *Delaware Coast Press*, the *Wave* and the *Salisbury Daily Times*. Morgan has also published articles in *Delaware Beach Life*, *America's Civil War*, the *Baltimore Sun*, *Chesapeake Bay Magazine*, *Civil War Times*, *Maryland Magazine*, *World War II Magazine* and other national publications. His "Lore of Delmarva" weekly radio commentary on historical topics relating to the Maryland and Delaware is broadcast by station WGMD 92.7. Morgan's look at history is marked by a lively storytelling style that has made his writing and lectures popular. Michael Morgan is also the author of *Pirates and Patriots, Tales of the Delaware Coast*; *Rehoboth Beach, A History of Surf and Sand*; *Bethany Beach, A Brief History*; *Ocean City, Going Down the Ocean*; *Civil War Delaware*; *Hidden History of Lewes*; *Delmarva's Patty Cannon*; *The Devil on the Nanticoke*; *World War II and the Delaware Coast*; *Storms that Shaped the Delmarva Coast*; and *Prohibition Delaware*. Morgan was inducted into the Delaware Maritime Hall of Fame in 2021.

Visit us at
www.historypress.com